# BERNADETTE OF LOURDES

'The simpler one writes, the better
it will be. In trying to dress things
up, one only distorts them.'

*Saint Bernadette on her deathbed, April 1879*

# BERNADETTE OF LOURDES

*A Life Based on Authenticated Documents*

RENÉ LAURENTIN

Introduction by Michael Hollings

Translated by John Drury

DARTON·LONGMAN + TODD

First published in Great Britain in 1979 by Darton, Longman and Todd Ltd

This edition published in 1998 by
Darton, Longman and Todd
1 Spencer Court
140–142 Wandsworth High Street
London SW18 4JJ

Reprinted 1999 and 2001

Originally published as *Vie de Bernadette* by Desclée De Brouwer, Paris

Translation © Winston Press

ISBN 0–232–52293–6

A catalogue record for this book is available from the British Library

Printed and bound in Great Britain by
Page Bros, Norwich, Norfolk

# CONTENTS

### 1
## LOURDES (1844–1866)

### 2
## NEVERS (JULY 7, 1866–APRIL 16, 1879)

# ABBREVIATIONS

This book is addressed to the general public, so references have been reduced to the minimum. The references used refer readers to basic works in which they will find the substantive basis and proof for what is written here, as well as detailed supplementary material. Thus the following list of abbreviations will also serve as a basic bibliography of essential works on the life of Bernadette and the apparitions at Lourdes.

A
: File A of Cros Archives. I cite mainly A III, A VI and A VII: Minutes of the 1878–80 investigation.

ANDL
: *Annales de Notre-Dame de Lourdes.*

Arch.
: Archives.

AZUN
: T. M. J. Azun de Bernétas, *La Grotte des Pyrénées*, Tarbes, Larrieu, 1961.

B
: R. Laurentin, *Bernadette vous parle*, Paris, Lethielleux, 1972, 2 volumes. A detailed life.

BARBET
: J. Barbet, *Bernadette Soubirous*, Pau, 1909. I cite the Tarbes edition of 1923.

CROS
: L. J. M. Cros, *Histoire de N. D. de Lourdes*, Paris, Beauchesne, 1927, 3 volumes.

D
: R. Laurentin, *Lourdes, documents authentiques* (in collaboration with B. Billet), 7 volumes, Paris, Lethielleux, 1957–66.

ESB
: A. Ravier, *Écrits de Saints Bernadette*, Paris, Lethielleux, 1961.

GUYNOT    E. Guynot, *Sainte Bernadette*. The numbers which follow this name indicate the date of various editions, in which the material chosen is varied.

H    R. Laurentin, *Lourdes, histoire authentique des apparitions*, 6 volumes, Paris, Lethielleux, 1961–4. The basis for the apparitions.

L    R. Laurentin and M. T. Bourgeade, *Logia de Bernadette*, 3 volumes, Paris, Lethielleux, 1971. A critical study of her words and sayings from 1866 to 1879. The number which follows the (L) indicates the *number of the saying in question*. The page is indicated afterwards only when there is good reason for doing so.

OG    M. Olphe-Galliard, *Lourdes 1858. Témoins de l'événement*, Paris, Lethielleux, 1957.

R    R. Laurentin, *Récit authentique des apparitions*, Paris, Lethielleux, 1966. An abridged version of H.

RC    Registre des contemporains, 1907, Nevers Archives. Register of Bernadette's contemporaries.

RSL    *Recherches dur Lourdes*, compiled in Lourdes by B. Billet.

V    B. Billet, *Bernadette, Une vocation* ... 2nd edition, Paris, Lethielleux, 1965.

[ ]    Indicates an addition of mine to a cited document.

FORCADE    A. Forcade (Bishop of Nevers in Bernadette's time), *Notice sur la vie de Soeur Marie-Bernard*. Aix, Makaíre, 1879.

LHA    As H above.

PANev    *Procès apostolique de béatification*, Nevers, 1917–19. 8 volumes. Nevers Archives and Vatican Secret Archives.

PATarb    *Procès apostolique de béatification*, Tarbes,

1915–19. Nevers Archives and Vatican Secret Archives.

PONev    *Procès de l'Ordinaire pour la béatification de Bernadette*, 1908–9. 6 volumes. Archives of the Sisters of Nevers and Vatican Secret Archives.

SEMPÉ    R. Sempé and Duboé, *Notre-Dame de Lourdes par ses premiers chapelains*, Paris, Letouzey, 9th edition, 1931.

VEDERE    *Bernadette et Jeanne Védère*, ed. Auros, 1933.

Photographs are taken from the collections of R. Laurentin, Von Matt, Durand and Viron.

# AUTHOR'S NOTE

This account has not been fictionalized. The names, the events, the dialogues and the quotes have been drawn scrupulously from authenticated documents. Fictitious elements, which still abound today in many works, have been excluded. The correctness of each detail can be verified in my other books, where I have tried to authenticate the account of the apparitions and the life of Bernadette: *Lourdes, documents authentiques* (D); *Lourdes, histoire authentique des apparitions* (H); and *Logia de Bernadette* (L). I use abbreviations to refer to these volumes and to others. The full list of these abbreviations can be found at the beginning of the book.

Here I would also like to say a brief word about the local dialect or *patois* of Lourdes. Up to the time of the apparitions Bernadette spoke only 'the *patois* of Lourdes', as she called it. It is in this dialect of the *langue d'oc* group that she received the communications of the Virgin Mary. For the sake of authenticity the following account records a few typical expressions in that dialogue that are indispensable to our story.

But how are we to transcribe that dialect? It is a hotly disputed question between two schools of thought: the *École Occitane* (the *langue d'oc* school) and the École Gaston Fébus. The orthography of the two schools differs, and neither coincides with the graphemes improvised for the contemporary documents. In another work, *Lourdes, histoire authentique* (H), I explored these issues in some détail and tried to settle them. In that work the reader will find that each utterance of the Virgin Mary is examined and that some confirmation is sought between the orthography of the *sources* and the transcriptions based on the principles of the two schools. My present work, however, is addressed to the public at large and so we cannot tackle such problems here. I have chosen to transcribe the *patois* as close to the documents as possible. However, I have adopted two specific conventions to obviate the controversies that always abound in matters of local parlance, be it in the case of La Salette, Lourdes or Pontmain:

1. I use the *accent-mark* only as a stress accent. This usage was unknown in Bernadette's day, but it is imperative today. If I were to use grave (`` ` ``) or acute (´) accents, I would be reproached by specialists whose competence I respect.

2. Hence the reader should remember that in the *langue d'oc* group of languages, and particularly in the dialect of Lourdes, there is no mute 'e'. It is to be pronounced at all times, with an acute or a grave accent as the case may be (é or è). This point is especially important in trying to avoid confusion over the word *Aquerò* ('that one') used by Bernadette to allude to the apparition (see p. 46).

Here I would like to thank Father Point and the members of the Missionaries of the Immaculate Conception, natives of Lourdes, who examined my transcriptions and gave me the benefit of their knowledge.

*Bernadette in 1864*

# INTRODUCTION

The pilgrim-visitor to Lourdes is drawn through busy streets, edged and crowded with shops selling every conceivable object of piety, to the comparative peace and prayerfulness of the 'domain' which insulates the area round the grotto of the apparitions.

There, standing, kneeling or sitting, the pilgrim faces the statue of the Virgin Mary placed in a niche of the rock. He or she has come to gaze upon that 'beautiful lady' whom a small girl called Bernadette reported as appearing and speaking with her in the year 1858.

Today, the image of the beautiful lady remains, but the figure of the small, poor and sick child Bernadette has disappeared. You and I, the pilgrims, take her place in looking towards the niche in the rock—and in doing so, as like as not, forget her. We are taken up with the beautiful lady who is now for us Our Lady.

But ... if we forget Bernadette we are liable to miss the meaning of Lourdes and much deep meaning in the Gospel story.

The facts of the story are that Bernadette, who died on April 16, 1879, was in human terms a most unlikely person to receive an apparition. At the time, owing to her father's poverty, they had lost almost everything and were housed in the old town gaol. Bernadette was young, poor, scarcely educated and of uncertain health. When, four years after the apparitions and with considerable reserve, the local Bishop came to recognize the authenticity of the apparitions he wrote in the official letter (January 18, 1862):

> What sort of instrument is the Almighty going to use to communicate his merciful designs to us? Once again it is what is poorest and most fragile in the world: a child of fourteen ... born ... of a poor family.

When she died at the age of thirty-five, twenty-one years after the apparitions, she had already virtually disappeared. While crowds were flocking to the grotto at Lourdes, Bernadette had been for thirteen years a nun. She died miles away in the convent of Saint-Gildard, Nevers.

She had deliberately hidden, but news of her death brought crowds to see her in her coffin. When after beatification on August 5, 1925 her body was exhumed intact, it was placed lying in state in a reliquary, and ever since that time crowds upon crowds of people from all over the world have come to pray and file past. So great was the popular devotion that Pope Pius XI canonized her on December 8, 1933, less than fifty years after her death, when, had she lived, she would have been eighty-nine.

Yet she had hidden, and we may perhaps get a glimpse at one practical reason which occurred as early as March 1858. A young girl, Antoinette Tardhivail, who herself was too sick to follow her Carmelite vocation, wrote her impression:

> Her parents are very poor ... as poor as Our Lord was on earth. And it is on this child that Mary has cast her gaze in preference to all the rich young people. Now, at this moment, they envy the lot of her whom they might otherwise have regarded with disdain; and they count themselves fortunate to be able to embrace her or touch her hand (Letter, March 29, 1858. D 5, p. 77).

Given a different character, and one which Mary would

find at odds with her own humble hiddenness in the life of Christ, Bernadette could have become a distraction to the crowds, who were called to the grotto not for the excitement of meeting a girl visionary, but for prayer and penance.

You may say after reading this far: Why then bother to write about her when she was always trying to hide and get out of God's way? The answer is as simple as the lesson we may learn from her if we look closely at her life: Bernadette is an example of holiness for our time. In a busy rushing world, where so much humanly depends upon getting on, passing examinations, achieving a higher income, surrounding oneself with comforts and luxuries beyond the dreams of two-thirds of the world, she lives poorly, asks for nothing but God's love, achieves nothing but her response to that love. She epitomizes the current catch-phrase 'small is beautiful'. She follows the hiddenness of Jesus in Nazareth and the retiring, faithful service of Mary, her beautiful lady.

It is easy for us to read these things. It is not easy to live them. For instance, her own mistress of novices, who was a remarkable and holy person in her own way, got fed up with talk about Bernadette's canonization. They were both living the life in the cloister and at close proximity the very ordinariness of living the rule may obscure the depth of giving of self which God draws out from individual souls.

Bernadette herself sensed the simplicity of the truth when she once said: 'The passion touches me more when I read it than when someone explains it to me' (L 576). The author of this book has tried to follow her advice to would-be historians of Lourdes: 'The more simply one writes, the better it will be ... In trying to dress things up, one only distorts them' (L 550 and 576).

And so the text as closely as possible follows the report of her life, her actions and her words. As much as possible is from the authentic documents. From these there comes forth a transparent simplicity, humility and truthfulness. Bernadette's attitude in the severe questioning at all ecclesiastical levels makes us want to use Jesus' own words of praise: 'Father, Lord of heaven and earth, to you I offer praise; for what you have hidden from the learned and the clever you have revealed to merest children' (Mt 11:25; Lk 10:21).

As we read her story, may the Lord touch us with her simplicity and love, for he loves each of us if only we will respond. If we accept our own nature in humility, each of us in his or her own way can echo Bernadette from the hidden depth of our souls:

> How happy was my soul, Good Mother, when I had the good fortune to gaze upon you . . . Yes, you stooped down to earth to appear to a mere child ... you deigned to make use of the most fragile thing in the world's eyes (ESB, p. 187).

And in echoing Bernadette, we are taken right back to the Gospel and to the central mystery of the Incarnation ... the God who gives himself in and through humility:

> God who is might has done great things for me. For he has looked upon his servant in her lowliness: all ages to come shall call me blessed (Lk 1:49).

By reading the story of Bernadette we touch the truth of humility.

*Michael Hollings*

# 1

# LOURDES
## (1844–1866)

*Childhood*
*The Apparitions*
*The Witness*

*Mill district: below, Savy*

*Savy Mill*

# BERNADETTE'S CHILDHOOD
# (1844–1858)

Bernadette Soubirous was born on January 7, 1844 in Boly, the next-to-last of five mills spaced some metres apart along the meagre brook of Lapaca, lying between the huge crag capped by the castle-fortress and the hilly meadows and woodlands rising gently towards Bartrès.

## A love marriage

There was joy in the mill. Bernadette was very much a wanted child. Her birth was the crowning touch to a love marriage, which had come about as the result of a calamity. Here is the story behind it.

On July 1, 1841 Justin Castérot, the miller of Boly, was killed in a cart accident on the Pouyferré road. His widow, Claire, stood before the corpse, spattered with flour, that was about to be buried. It was time to give some serious thought to her problem. She had four grown daughters and two young children in the mill, whose wheel had now stopped turning. The dead man had thought he was the proprietor at least, but he was nothing of the sort. These uneducated people did not in the least understand a complicated situation, whose only clear feature was their obligation to pay an annual *fiou* of 130 francs-or.

The eldest daughter, Bernarde, aged 19, would have to be married off quickly to some bachelor in the guild. The widow Castérot made overtures to François Soubirous of the Latour mill, who was still single at the age of 34. He did not require much coaxing, and came readily to the mill, smiling and affable. But there was no progress as far as the marriage was concerned. What was going on behind that amiable but stubborn forehead?

Finally they guessed. The one who 'interested' François was not Bernarde but her younger sister, Louise, with her blonde hair and blue eyes. When he was forced to acknowledge this anomaly, François avoided offering any reasons based on affection or love. They had no place in the mill trade of nineteenth-century Lourdes.

'Louise is a better housekeeper,' argued François.

The evidence was all to the contrary. Bernarde was a woman with a good head and an air of authority if there ever was one. Louise was only 17: she was too young. It would not be proper to marry her off before the eldest. François offered no reply to these arguments. He just sat there, smiling wearily. The family had to take his part after all, because he would marry Louise or no one.

### A birth

The wedding took place on January 9, 1843 and Bernadette was born on January 7 of the following year. The next day François, proud but awkward, carried the infant to the town hall, as was the custom. Baptism took place the day after that, January 9, her parents' first wedding anniversary.

Bernadette was baptized in the old granite baptistery where inhabitants of Lourdes are baptized even to this day. She cried during the ceremony. Was it perhaps a presentiment of the strange promise she would be given later: that she would 'not be happy in this world'? Another symbol points in the same direction. The most familiar

noise to her in those first years was the sound of the millstones and the grain being ground. On her deathbed she
would identify herself with the latter: 'I have been ground
in the mill like wheat.'

The festive celebration of January 9, 1844 left this simple memory, recorded much later in the *patois* of Lourdes:
*Uo tisto de crespèts, è bouteilles de pichè sus era taoulo. On
fit une ronde.* It is easy enough to picture the scene: The
people around the table, and on it a big basket (*tisto*) of
fritters (*crespèts*) and large bottles that can hold from two
to three litres (*bouteilles de pichè*).

## The heir

Five women were available to watch over Bernadette's
cradle, ranging from the grandmother to little Aunt
Lucile, aged 4. The person in charge was Bernarde, 'the
heir'. For according to the custom in the county of Bigorre
the firstborn, whether male or female, bore this title and
this honour. It did not matter whether there was any
inheritance or not. The opinion of the firstborn prevailed
over that of the younger children, both the males and
females. Bernadette, too, was born 'the heir'. In that
capacity she would always remain conscious of her duties
to her family.

The love which surrounded Bernadette's infancy
remained with her throughout her life. It was one of those
deep roots that grace knows how to use to fashion saints.

Her mother, Louise, was gentle and patient. With her
happy marriage she had usurped her sister's privilege, and
she felt somewhat abashed by it all. She willingly shared
her baby without recriminations. 'She knew me as well as
she knew her mother,' said Aunt Bernarde proudly.

But the touchstone for Bernadette was the silent, smiling man of the mill, her father, who was proud of his
firstborn. In the eyes of the new 'heir', the royal image of
her infancy was his white-powdered beret and his eyes

gazing on her tenderly. (At that point François Soubirous still had both his eyes intact.)

Thus a deep sense of security took root in Bernadette. It would remain with her, indestructible, in the face of blasts that could have shattered rock. Indeed the results could have been fatal for her if these fundamental supports had not been there, symbolizing for her another and deeper reality that was evoked each evening by the murmur of rough peasant voices before sleep came: 'Our Father, who art in heaven. . . .' It was the time of day when the noise of the millstones had ceased and the gurgle of the brook gradually rose amid the silence.

Bernadette did not know that her name, Soubirous, meant 'Sovereign'. But a sovereign image, that of God, inhabited her childhood and her life of simplicity close to nature. It gave her that spirited dignity combined with humility which characterized her whole person.

### Bartrès

Misfortune did not wait for Bernadette to complete her first year. One November evening in 1844 Louise, again pregnant, was sitting in a corner of the fireplace. The resin candle hanging from the chimney fell on her and when she came to, she was in flames. There was no longer any question of nursing Bernadette at her burnt breasts.

Aunt Bernarde went out looking for a wet-nurse. In Bartrès, on the very hill whose slopes descend to the mill, it so happened that Marie Laguës had just lost her firstborn son, Jean, eighteen days old. She readily agreed to nurse Bernadette, taking charge of her for five francs a month payable in silver or in cereal grain. Aunt Bernarde stayed up on the hill for eight days with the baby so that she might grow accustomed to the place more easily.

But Bernadette's most assiduous visitor was François. Before this no one had ever seen him so much on the steep uphill path to Bartrès, a distance of four kilometres. Now suddenly there was grain to pick up, flour to deliver, or clients to badger and woo. Soon he began to drop hints about taking back his daughter. Marie Laguës resisted. She had become attached to the baby and could not reconcile herself to the sight of an empty crib. But the crib in the Boly mill was empty too. Little Jean Soubirous, born on February 13, 1845, died on April 10. And Bernadette was weaned by December 1845.

Marie Laguës held out. She would watch the baby *for free*. She returned her only on April 1, 1846, when she was sure of a new and eagerly awaited pregnancy. All these dealings took place in the slow and ceremonious forms typical of peasant courtesy. When Louise Soubirous came to pick up her daughter, she brought a handkerchief as a gift for this formal occasion. In the springtime Bernadette, now two years and four months old, rediscovered the sound of the millstones and the rushing water. They had now become a danger for her as she toddled around with curious and independent steps.

**Good times and bad at Boly Mill**

In 1848 a separation took place between the Soubirous household, which had been under tutelage, and the Castérot clan. Bernarde, seduced by Tarbès, had become a mother before the parents of her swain had authorized the marriage. Claire Castérot left the mill, taking her unmarried children with her. François and Louise was surprised suddenly to find themselves alone in the mill like two lovers. How free and easy life became when one was not subject to glances, constraints and counsels every minute!

Another event could not have escaped Bernadette's notice. François Soubirous was 'dressing' his millstones, which had become too smooth, when he suddenly stopped and let out a yell. He came in, his hand over his face, his left eye cut from a direct blow. The eye was lost. Henceforth he was reduced to hiding his infirmity by keeping the eyelid half-shut, as his photos show, in order to spare others the sight of this disgrace.

## The Passion of the Soubirous family

Were the Soubirous destined to relive the fate of Job? Money was short at the mill. They found it hard to understand why. They worked hard at it and, even with competition, there was always a customer. The reason was that these good people were just a bit too kind-hearted to be good managers in hard times. They opened their doors readily to beggars, including one Michel Garicoïts. They showed compassion for those who were insolvent, advancing them grain and flour 'until the coming harvest' without haggling.

'You will pay when you can,' said Louise.

To customers who came to bring grain or pick up flour the miller's wife served a collation: a little wine, a little cheese, and sometimes some 'fritters' like those served at the time of Bernadette's baptism. She was a great hand at making them. And why should they keep tabs on oil and flour when there was so much of it? So the atmosphere was gay and animated, but the returns were poor. This state of things drove away the 'serious' clientele and attracted the 'bad' customers: those who didn't pay. It became harder and harder to pay their bills when they fell due.

In 1854, the year that Bernadette turned 10 and that Pius IX defined the dogma of Mary's Immaculate Conception, the family had to break up their household. Bernadette left the happy mill of her early childhood.

The furniture was transported to the Laborde home, and François began to look around for precarious jobs in order to win bread for his four children. For after Bernadette, Louise had given birth to three more children: Toinette (1846), Jean-Marie (1851), and Justin (February 28, 1855).

No longer a miller, François had become a *brassier*, a 'day-labourer' who hired out his arm (*bras*) and was paid for his brute strength. The average daily pay for a man was 1.20 francs, less than that for a horse or a mule. Rental of the latter had risen to 1.55 francs per day.

According to statistics in the *Indicateur des Hautes Pyrénées* (Paris 1856), a family of five needed an annual income of 523 francs at least for their bare subsistence. There were six in the Soubirous family. Counting Sundays, feast days, holidays and days without work, they were far below the mark.

Louise, too had begun to work: housekeeping, washing, and work in the fields. Bernadette took care of Justin. When he was hungry and cried, she carried him to his mother in the fields. There, in the shade of the bales, his mother offered her nipple and the baby sucked what milk was left in the ill-nourished woman who was dried out by her harsh labour under the hot sun of early summer. Of the nine children that she eventually brought into the world, five did not survive to the age of ten.

When Louise was unemployed, the two eldest children went out to gather wood, bones, or scrap-iron. They hunted for anything that the rag-picker Letchina de Barràou might be willing to buy for a few pennies. She in turn would sell them to the big scrap-dealer: Casteret. School was out of the question for Bernadette.

In the autumn of 1855, a cholera epidemic broke out in Lourdes, unleashing terrible attacks of diarrhoea that dehydrated people in a matter of hours and reduced them to corpses. There were eight deaths on September 23, thirty on October 10. Calamity, which prompts some human beings to take to their heels, also reveals those with a courageous heart. Father Peyramale, the new parish priest and dean who had come to Lourdes the previous March, was one of the latter. So was Commissioner Jacomet, who went everywhere to fill the breach with his friend, Sergeant D'Angla. They vied with each other in rubbing down the sick with wisps of straw, which was the prevailing treatment at Lourdes. Bernadette just managed to escape the epidemic but her health, which had become frailer since her sixth birthday, deteriorated even further. Despite the recipes of Rosine Haillet, the midwife, her asthma never left her.

On October 22, 1855 Claire Castérot, Bernadette's maternal grandmother, died. She had escaped the epidemic too, but later died and was buried fourteen years after the death of her husband. Her death restored the financial situation of the Soubirous family. Thanks to her frugality, the Soubirous inherited 900 francs. They purchased a few head of livestock, hoping to begin again with some calves, some cows, some hogs and some stock hatched from eggs. Investing more than they had, they rented the Sarrabeyrouse mill on the Echez, in the village of Arcizac-ès-Angles, about four kilometres from Lourdes. But the contract signed by the illiterate François Soubirous was ruinous. He barely managed to stick to it for one year. At the first expiration date of the contract they were forced to set out again. François could no longer nurture the foolish hope of ever renting a mill again.

They sank lower and lower. Their affection for one another was put to the test by the incontestable reality of their material situation: 'Too many mouths to feed,' as Bernadette was to put it (H2, p. 30, note 85). They would have to face up to the reality of the situation if they were to survive.

### The servant-girl

During the winter of 1856–7, the Soubirous resigned themselves to the idea of reducing by one the number of 'mouths to feed'. Bernadette's godmother, Aunt Bernarde, took her in as a little servant-girl. Bernadette was to help her take care of the house and the café that she, Bernarde, had inherited from her first husband. It was situated on the corner of the Rue du Bourg and the Rue du Baous.

Bernadette took care of her cousins, did the washing, mended the clothes, did the needlework at which she excelled, and served at the counter. She submitted to the firm authority of Aunt Bernarde, who ran things with a stick when she had to; but Bernadette was inclined to display the same generosity that characterized her parents when they lived in the Boly mill. Her generosity was stronger than her exemplary docility. She had a knack of filling the measuring cup on the counter in such a way that a gulp was left at the bottom when she had filled a bottle. And she would say to her friend Jeanne-Marie Caudeban (who tells the story) or others: 'Take a drink of that, Marie!' In Lourdes wine was relatively rare, and it was regarded as a tonic or a marvellous remedy.

**The Gaol**

At the start of 1857 the Soubirous were thrown on to the street again, with a little help from continuing unemployment. They were forced to quit their seedy lodging in the Rives house, leaving behind their wardrobe in pawn to the proprietor. Moving was becoming easier and easier, since their load was lighter each time. Where were they to find a roof over their heads? Where were they to find an even worse place that would take them in? No one wanted the Soubirous any more. The last chance open to them was the Gaol, which was described as 'a foul, sombre hovel' by Prosecutor Dutour in his report of March 1, 1858.

The Gaol was the scarcely habitable room of the old prison. The latter had been abandoned in 1824 because of its unhealthiness. Jean-Pierre Taillade purchased the building and had the bars removed from the windows, but did not eliminate the humidity or the stench of poultry manure. Uncle Taillade then leased the ramshackle building to André Sajous, a cousin of the Soubirous, during his lifetime. Sajous had cut out a second window, but it looked out on the same courtyard. Then François came knocking at his door. Sajous was honest in recalling his feelings at that moment:

> I was not happy about it! They had four children. I myself had five. I realized full well that my wife, a very kind woman, would give them some of our bread.
>
> I used to lodge Spaniards there. They came during the winter to do some digging work and would sleep there on the flagstones with their blankets over them. Often there was no straw.

These migrants from across the Pyrenees represented the ultimate degree of misery and poverty in Lourdes. They were 'a ragged band of Spaniards', as Zola describes them scornfully in his journal investigating Lourdes. The Soubirous had sunk to their level, as one story of that period indicates.

Little Amanda Jacomet, daughter of Commissioner Jacomet and five years old at the time, had finished her first piece of knitting: a pair of little white stockings. 'You should give them to the first poor child who comes along, even if it be a Spaniard,' said Madame Jacomet, who was a good-hearted woman. But the first to present himself was Bernadette's little brother—with no socks on his feet.

The Spaniards had left the Gaol towards the end of winter in 1856, but they would undoubtedly be back the following winter. Thus there would be a loss of income for Sajous. He put off his answer until the evening and went to talk the matter over with Uncle Taillade, who had bequeathed him the Gaol. The conclusion seemed inescapable: 'They are out on the street. We must give them lodging.'

In the sombre room, 3.72 metres by 4.40 metres, they did their best to squeeze in the meagre belongings of the Soubirous: two beds (three were really needed for six people), a table, two chairs, the children's stools, a small wardrobe and the trunk. The latter was now big enough to hold the family's clothes and linen, including their bed sheets. That much was their own. They quickly discovered the vermin of the preceding occupants.

## Famine

The course of wretched poverty had speeded up in 1856. On August 26, the Procurator General of Pau dispatched an alarming confidential report to Paris:

> The wheat crop is averaging out as a third of the normal harvest. Oidium (a vine-mildew), which has been decimating the grape harvest for three years, has now reached its peak. Corn, which was at 13 francs in May, is now at 27 francs. Wheat has risen to 42 francs.

Famine was on the horizon. The problem was doubly insoluble, notes the report, because there was no railroad to dispatch the wheat and no money among the poor population to purchase it. Hunger intensified at the Gaol. Bernadette played at making grass soups, which nourish only the imagination.

One day during this tragic winter Emmanuélite Estrade was praying in church. She was surprised by an unusual noise alongside the catafalques. What did she find? An unknown little boy was scraping off the wax that had fallen from the candles, as a little rat might; someone who is hungry will eat anything. The little boy would not tell her his name. But later, on February 23, 1858, during the period of the apparitions, Emmanuélite identified the small boy as Jean-Marie, Bernadette's little brother. Later on Jean-Marie was to forget and deny this childhood memory (H2, p. 224).

## François in prison

Immediately after that wretched winter was over, on

March 27, 1857, the police descended on the Gaol and
arrested François Soubirous as a malefactor. During the
preceding night two sacks of flour had been stolen from
Maisongrosse, the baker. He accused François Soubirous,
whom he had employed in September 1856 to deliver
flour to Luz. Maisongrosse spoke well of him: 'During the
time he was with me, I had no reason at all to complain
about his integrity.' But he added: 'It was his state of
misery that led me to believe that he might be the one
behind this theft' (Prosecutor's Report, March 21, 1857).

His line of reasoning made an impression on the police.
They confiscated the half-boots of the former miller and
took him barefoot to the baker's shop in order to carry on
their investigation. The prints of the robber were nearly
'the same size' as the half-boots, notes the report; but it
also points out that the setting of the nails is different.
François Soubirous added that 'the shape of the half-boots
was bigger than that of the prints'.

So was François released? No, because the search made
at his home turned up a thick plank of wood. Where did
that come from? François Soubirous grew rather uncertain
and confused. The plank had stood abandoned for a long
time against a wall on the Rue des Petits Fossés. He had
picked it up with his bundle of sticks on returning from
Bartrès. So while the flour wouldn't do the trick, the plank
gave the police the 'robbery' of which the impoverished
former miller had been suspected. He was put in gaol, and
the plank of wood was 'dropped off at the town hall', to be
returned to its 'owner' when that party put in an appearance. No one came to claim it, and for a good reason. The
following year it was to be used as the post to which the
authorities affixed their notice prohibiting people from
entering the grotto as of June 1858.

In prison François mused about his family. They had
been dragged into disgrace and they were even more
afflicted than he by hunger, for want of his daily pay.

On April 4, the Prosecutor terminated François' pre-
trial detention for 'humanitarian reasons', according to the
the report. The investigation was dropped for insufficient

grounds. But the reputation of the Soubirous had fallen even further. Because he was one-eyed and his affairs were going badly, François was regarded as an idler and an incompetent. 'He drinks,' added some people on the Castérot side of the family. 'It is she who drinks,' said some on the Soubirous side. There were no really solid grounds for the accusations, but weakness and undernourishment may at times have inclined them to prefer a glass of wine to a more 'normal' kind of nourishment in order to find new heart for the tasks facing them. At that time everyone in the area shared the current idea that wine 'provides strength' (LHA 1, pp. 77–80).

François had now fallen to the level of a common thief. Only two things were left to sustain his pride. First there was Louise, spirited and unreproachful. They remained united in their distress even as they had been in their good times. There were never 'words' between them: That was admitted even by members of the two families who had tried to set them at odds with each other.

And something else, over and above themselves, kept them united. Through the floor-boards Cousin Sajous heard the voices of the Soubirous 'bawling out' their evening prayer in French—a language which Bernadette did not understand (she spoke only the local dialect or *patois*). But through the obscure words she once again united with a Presence. She received it almost naturally, direct from the source. And it was a support for her in the fields of Bartrès.

## Bartrès (1857)

For Bernadette was back with her wet-nurse in September 1857. The reasons were commonplace enough. It was the same old problem really: one too many among the 'mouths to feed'. No matter how nice it was to be all together, one less around meant a little bit more for each present at mealtimes.

After March 1858, Bernadette's life in Bartrès was to

be enveloped in legend. Wondrous tales were to find their way into the newspapers, told in an admiring or ironic vein. Her flock had miraculously cleared a swollen stream in a storm, and they did not get wet from the rain, to the wonderment of all. Bernadette herself gave the lie to all these legends, much to the disappointment of her admirers.

Let us not be tempted into idealising the scene or the mysticism of the shepherdess. For Bernadette, Bartrès was no pastoral idyll, no sacred version of Marie Antoinette's Trianon, as some tourists like to imagine. Her meals were austere. Meat from the butcher's shop appeared on the table only twice a year: at Christmas and on the feast of Saint John. The regular morning and evening meal was the corn paste which Bernadette's stomach had turned against a long time ago. In her own home they would give her wheat bread for her portion, but in Bartrès that was 'the privilege of venerable, old masters'.

Moreover, Marie Laguës was harsh with her former suckling. She loved Bernadette after her own fashion, but she had never quite forgiven her for taking the milk from her dead little son, Jean. Then she lost a second little Jean, aged 2, on March 1, 1850. The third little Jean, who was now in Bernadette's care, was wasting away, and would not last through the autumn.

Bernadette was not only the shepherdess and the babysitter. She was also the little maid who was expected to do all the cleaning up as well as other chores. She was docile and never sulked about her work. What hurt her the most was the fact that she had come on the understanding that she would at last be able to study her catechism with Father Ader, the parish priest of Bartrès. But the place of a shepherdess is always with her sheep.

What was Bernadette's life like in Bartrès, where the gentle hills inspired dreams? Without a doubt it was one long solitude. But Bernadette would sometimes remedy the situation by inviting along a companion, Jeanne-Marie Caudeban, who was also a little servant-girl. When Bernadette was alone, she would play with her dog, Pigou, and with her lambs. She loved the 'littlest ones'. It was one point that remained clearly impressed on her memory right up to the very end of her life.

Bernadette liked to build little altars during the month of May, as was customary in that area. They helped her to pray. But her favourite lamb did not share her piety. He would charge her from behind and cause her knees to buckle, or else he would knock over the 'little altars'. Bernadette could not hold a grudge against him: 'To punish him, I would give him a little salt, of which he was very fond.'

She loved that friendly universe, to which she brought order and peace. Little incidents like the ones mentioned above were moments of diversion amid the interminable solitude.

Her father came up to visit her, just as he had done when she was a suckling infant. One day he found her very sad in the meadow.

'Look at my sheep. Some have a green back. What is the matter with them?'

His current misfortunes prompted a streak of wry humour in François: 'The grass they've eaten has got into their backs. They're going to die.'

Bernadette cried, but found no consolation. The green stripe was the butcher's mark: her sheep were indeed going to die.

Back at the house in the evening, her old nurse got it into her head to teach Bernadette her catechism. She was trying to allay her guilt feelings for having reneged on the promise that she had made, but her teaching was not on a par with her good intentions. She repeated the phrases in an imperative tone, hammering them out like blows: 'Say it again! Say it again!'

The words just would not stick in the head of the girl who had never attended school. Bernadette's understanding of things came from the inside, and she could not see any connection between the abstract phrases and the First Communion that she yearned to make. Her old nurse grew exasperated and ended up tossing the catechism across the room: 'Look! You are too stupid! You will never make your First Communion!'

Father Aravant, brother of Bernadette's former nurse, witnessed those scenes and remonstrated with his sister. 'She changed her approach for a while ... but then she went back to her usual style,' Bernadette confided to Jeanne Védère one day (H 2, p. 58). Without this confidential remark to her most intimate girlfriend, Bernadette would have left us nothing but words of praise and affection for her old nurse. It is through others that we learn of the unhappier side of Bernadette's life.

## When the good God permits it

Without another confidential remark to Jeanne, something else would remain unknown. This particular comment reveals to us one of the wellsprings of her patience and gentleness: 'When the good God permits it, one does not complain.' The remark is perfectly apt, right on target. Bernadette did not say, 'What God *wills*' when she was talking about sufferings and injustices endured. She found peace by adhering to her principle, but that did not keep her from looking for a happier way out.

Both Aunt Bernarde and her former nurse testified to Bernadette's gentleness and docility. But was she pious?

'Oh, like anybody else!' was the reply of Justine Laguës to Father Servais in 1913.

'I don't recall having seen her with a rosary,' said Jeanne-Marie Caudeban, her former companion in the Arribans meadow.

On her deathbed (December 12, 1878) Bernadette herself was asked whether she had recited the rosary in the fields of Bartrès.

'I don't remember that,' was her reply.

She had forgotten a great deal. Her mother, Louise Soubirous, noticed that from a very early age Bernadette showed 'a marked inclination towards piety' (Testimony of November 12, 1859; D5, p. 327). She liked to decorate little altars or shrines during the month of May, in honour of Mary, both at home near her bed and in the fields of Bartrès. But that was a local custom and there was nothing singular in her practice (H2, p. 60). She owned a rosary, which Toinette had bought for her in 1856, in Bétharram, for two sous (A7, p. 173). She could recite the rosary in French, though she only knew the language in a vague general way, as many Catholics were familiar with Latin before Vatican II (H2, p. 50). Indeed this rosary was in her pocket at the time of the first apparition, and fingering the beads was a familiar gesture for her. Bernadette also knew the invocation that was recited at their evening prayer: 'O Mary conceived without sin, pray for us who have recourse to thee.'

And there we have all that can be gathered from the investigators who explored Bartrès: some to find some miraculous origin, others—such as Zola—to pry out the secret of a dishevelled 'mysticism'.

## A spirituality hidden in simplicity

Bernadette was not a mystic in the vulgar sense, showing some peculiar or bizarre brand of fervour. Nor was she a mystic in the scholarly sense, displaying one of those spiritual states that are described in manuals of ascetic theology. And yet, for all that, she was quite advanced in the practice of true mysticism: i.e., of union with God. She lived it in the way that poor and lowly people do, in the way that thrilled Jesus Christ and caused him to exclaim: 'Father, Lord of heaven and earth, to you I offer praise; for what you have hidden from the learned and the clever you have revealed to the merest children' (Mt 11:25). What we are dealing with here is a quiet grace that has left no noisy echo in the journals or even in the archives. But the priests of that region encountered it often enough: a quiet contemplative experience evident among the shepherds or peasants of the area.

When it comes to dealing with the holiness of the poor and lowly, one must know how to catch the slightest hint beneath a veil of silence or half-spoken words. Bernadette's parents were too quiet for us to be able to say anything about their 'religious experience', their generosity of heart, or their wholehearted agreement that foiled all attempts to set them against one another. But many visitors were sensitive enough to catch a glimmer of all this: those who did not just come to cavil and raise questions but who were wise enough to intuit the reality of living beings and their circumstances. Azun de Bernétas noted down his first impressions upon entering the Gaol on November 12, 1859:

> On entering the Soubirous home, one is struck by the same family air that pervades all the faces. Peace, innocence and happiness seem to shine out from the placid features that typify all of them. And yet they are indigent in every sense of the word.... How happy we were in the midst of those blessed little ones! (D5, p. 328).

Following in their footsteps, Bernadette lived the Gospel message on good authority, without any high-flown knowledge or idle chatter. She forgot many things very quickly. Her right hand did not know what her left hand was doing, and she was a complete stranger to any and every sort of spiritual exhibitionism. She discouraged all those who sought to probe deeper than her simplicity in trying to pinpoint her secret.

She lived her union with God at all times, amid a dearth of words and means. She lived it in the communion of saints, of the saints on earth and in heaven, whose presence seemed so close to the people of her day. John the Baptist lit up the church of Bartrès from his gilded bas-relief overhead. Saint Peter did the same for the church in Lourdes. The Virgin Mary shed her gentle light on both churches.

But the holiness of Bernadette lay outside the bounds of

any religious instruction. She did not even have any fam-
iliarity with the mystery of the Holy Trinity. Father
Pomian was quick to register his realization of this fact and
his shocked surprise. Bernadette was a stranger to all
reflective awareness. She lived a spiritual night. To put it
plainly and simply, it was the night of the '*pauvres*', the
'poor little ones' who await the Good News while carrying
out the 'will of God' and enduring what he permits, as
Bernadette suggested to Jeanne Védère in her confidential
remark.

## Return to the Gaol

Resignation to the will of God did not stop Bernadette
from thinking about her plight and trying to work out a
solution. She began to put her thinking into practice at the
end of 1857, when she went down every Sunday to greet
her own family.

On December 5 of that year it was the turn of the third
little Jean Laguës to die. His death reopened the wound
inflicted on the heart of Bernadette's wet-nurse thirteen
years earlier. The atmosphere of the house grew very
oppressive, as the grief-stricken mother worked her emotions off on Bernadette. The hope of catechism lessons,
put off from one Thursday to the next, was now squelched
altogether. On January 3, 1858, Father Ader, the parish
priest of Bartrès, said farewell to the parish house after
presiding over his last baptism, his last marriage, and a
final meeting of the parish council. He was leaving for
Pierre-qui-Vire to pursue his attraction to the Benedictine
way of life. No one yet knew who his replacement would
be.

Bernadette had made up her mind. Now she must get
other people to accept her decision. She informed her
parents that she was 'sick and tired' in Bartrès. Coming
from one who weighed her words so carefully, the phrase
made an impact. Françoise Soubirous understood her dis-

tress. Her mother agreed. The process of leaving Bartrès got under way gently.

On Sunday, January 17, 1858, Bernadette was going down to Lourdes as she did every Sunday, bringing with her a few potatoes that were a real blessing. On her way out of the house in Bartrès, she withdrew into the silence of her shell when her old nurse spoke her usual parting word: 'You will be back this evening, without fail.'

Bernadette did not reappear that day, nor the next day, nor the day after that. It was Wednesday before she returned, with a clearcut and well-prepared response on her lips: 'Reverend Father, the parish priest, wants me to make my First Communion.'

Who could contest the decision of the Reverend Father, seeing that there was now no parish priest in Bartrès? Bernadette was then past her fourteenth birthday, and the Laguës were feeling guilty. For one last time Bernadette borrowed Jeanne-Marie Caudeban's handkerchief while she washed her own. She would start for home the next day, Thursday, with her meagre luggage.

Farewell to her girlfriends, Jeanne-Marie Caudeban and Jeanne-Marie Garros. Farewell to her foster-brothers, Zéphirin, Joseph and Justin. Farewell to papa Laguës, the good soul of the house. Farewell to her old nurse, whose affection always resurfaced at arrivals and departures.

Bernadette turned her back on the Burg house. She turned left after the church and curtseyed to the cross at the junction in passing. The road she took then was not the road that has been opened since for tourists. It was a cart-road with deep, twisting ruts that ran along the edge of the plateau before descending to the Gave river. The dark inclines of the north slope on her right did not draw her attention. On the opposite side, which saw no sun in winter, Bernadette did not notice the sheer cliff of old rock known as the *Masse vieille*—or Massabieille in the *Patois* of Lourdes. Indeed was Bernadette even acquainted with the name of that rocky recess, which was difficult of access and had a bad reputation, and which served as grazing ground for the township's herd of swine? If she was, in all likelihood it was through the old question bandied about in the area: 'Have you climbed the Massabielle?' The question itself shed little light on the subject, and Bernadette herself had never been there. At the end of the right fork, the road descended into Lourdes. There was the steeple of the parish church where she would at last learn her catechism and make her First Communion.

Back in the Gaol she once again discovered the poverty, the dampness, the stench and the gloominess. But she also had the affection of her own family once again. It was the choice that she herself had made.

*François Soubirous*   *Bernadette's mother, Louise*

*The Gaol*

2

# THE FIRST THREE APPARITIONS
## (FEBRUARY 11, 14, 18)

Thursday, February 11, 1858, was a day like any other in the Gaol. The loathsome atmosphere passed unnoticed because the occupants were used to it. It was 11:00 a.m. François Soubirous was lying in bed because there was no work for him that day. He was saving his strength for the next day, or the day after that.

'Good heavens, there's no more wood!' exclaimed Bernadette.

The scheme was put in hand. Toinette wanted to go too; and in came Jeanne Abadie, known as Baloum, the quarryman's daughter, a big, brash girl who acted quite grown up. She let it be known that she would go too.

'Not Bernadette,' said May (Bernadette's mother).

Outside there was mist and a drizzling rain. Louise was afraid that the cold and damp would not do her eldest daughter's asthma any good. But Bernadette pleaded and insisted. Breathless in the close atmosphere of the Gaol, she longed for the open air. Permission was granted, along with many words of warning and advice. May fastened a white hood on Bernadette's head. It was a well patched bonnet that she bought second-hand on the Marcadal, the municipal square.

**Looking for wood**

The three pairs of wooden clogs echoed on the paving

stones of the Rue des Petits Fossés, then on the arch of the
Baous gate that opened out on to the countryside. There
was hardly anything to pick up in Paradise meadow that
ran alongside the cemetery. It was too close to town. The
three little rag-pickers descended towards the Pont Vieux.
There old Pigoune was washing some purplish guts.

'Auntie, what are you doing there? Who are you washing those guts for?'

'It's Monsieur Clarens's pig. And what are you lot doing
here in this bad weather?'

'We're looking for wood.'

Go to Monsieur La Fitte's meadow. He's cut down
some trees.'

'No!' protests Bernadette. 'We'd be taken for thieves
. . .'

'Stay on the Massabielle side.'

300 metres further on, the girls crossed the bridge over
the canal which turned the Savy mill. It leads them into the
meadow—an island between the canal and the Gave—
with which they were not familiar. Nicolau, the Savy miller, came out on his doorstep. He didn't care to see the
three little foragers picking their way through the freshly
cut wood.

'Hey, rascals! Don't touch the wood!'

They hastened their step, keeping calm; but they didn't
gather any of the branches that lay all over the ground. All
over the meadow poplars were standing like skeletons,
denuded of their branches.

'Let's go and see where the canal rejoins the Gave,'
proposed Bernadette.

'And what if it joins it at Bétharram?' exclaimed
Toinette, who liked to contradict the 'heir'.

The exploration did not take long. 200 metres farther
on, they came to the sandy point where the Gave rejoined
the channel of the mill, which wasn't working that day. To
their left was a rocky cliff with a grotto carved out of it at
the bottom. The water of the canal washed its left side.
Among the rocks and moraines that ascended over the
grotto the foragers saw wood and old bones. They had

found hardly anything at all so far.

Jeanne threw her clogs to the other side and crossed, holding her bundle of sticks on her head. Toinette followed her, holding her sticks in her hand. Bernadette was left alone on the other bank with her asthma and her mother's cautions.

'Help me to throw some stones in the water so that I can cross!'

The two others were engrossed in their foraging.

'Pet de périclé! Cross over like we did!' shouted Jeanne.

*Pet de périclé* was a favourite little swear-word of her father, akin to 'thunderation!' in English. Jeanne was vexed with the lazy creature who had not gathered as much as she and Toinette.

## A gust of wind

Bernadette was looking for a way to get across. No luck.

'Then,' she wrote, 'I came back opposite the grotto and I began to take off my shoes and stockings. I had just removed the first stocking when I heard a noise something like a gust of wind.'

Bernadette looked behind her. The poplars were not moving. She bent over to take off the second stocking. The same noise again! But this time she saw branches moving directly across from her. They were the branches of a wild rosebush (*Rosa canina*) rooted in the bottom of a niche of some sort. It was growing in three metres of earth, above the right edge of the grotto. A 'gentle light' brightened the dark recess and there, in the light, was a smile. There stood a wonderfully beautiful girl, dressed in white. She opened her hands in a welcoming gesture that seemed to invite Bernadette to come closer. Bernadette was seized with a kind of 'fear,' but 'not to run away.' On the contrary, she would have liked nothing better than to remain there. Bernadette struggled to make sure she was not dreaming. She blinked her eyes several times. But each time she again saw the same apparition and the same smile. Then, she tells us:

> I put my hand in my pocket, and I found my rosary there. I wanted to make the Sign of the Cross.... I couldn't raise my hand to my forehead. It collapsed on me. Shock got the better of me. My hand was trembling.
> The vision made the Sign of the Cross. Then I tried a second time, and I could. As soon as I made the Sign of the Cross, the fearful shock I felt disappeared. I knelt down and I said my rosary in the presence of the beautiful lady. The vision fingered the beads of her own rosary, but she did not move her lips. When I finished my rosary, she signed for me to approach; but I did not dare. Then she disappeared, just like that.

There was nothing there now but the sombre rock and the drizzling rain. Happy but far from starry-eyed, Bernadette went back to her problems where she had left them: one stocking on, one stocking off. She found her second stocking down round her ankle and took it off. Then she crossed the stream without any difficulty. She sat down on one of the bigger stones among the pebbles, right on the threshold of the grotto.

### A confidence betrayed

Her two companions came back. Heading downstream along the left bank, they had seen Bernadette in prayer. Baloum had shrugged her shoulders: 'It's silly to pray there. Praying in church is quite enough!'

Now they were back with a good load of wood. Sheltered from the rain under the roof of the grotto, they danced about to warm up. Bernadette didn't like to see them frisking about there.

'Did you see anything?' she asked suddenly.

'What about you, what did *you* see?'

Bernadette realized the mysteriousness of the thing that had happened to her. She had to keep it to herself, and so she shifted the conversation to something else.

'You jokers, you told me that the water was cold. But I found it very mild.'

Jeanne Abadie was tying up her bundle of wood. Bernadette inspected the grotto again. She looked at the massive cliff with its many caverns; the pebbly ground, brown for the most part but sprinkled here and there with specks of red; the bramble-bush, stock still in the empty niche. She could not help but ask again.

'Did you see anything?'

'What about you, what did you see?'

'Oh, nothing' (*Labets, arré*: H2, p. 181).

Toinette was becoming intrigued, but Jeanne was getting annoyed.

'She hasn't seen anything at all. She just didn't want to gather any wood! May will give her a good scolding!'

Jeanne loaded her bundle of wood on her head and grabbed her basket of bones. She disappeared into the brushwood along the hillside, leaving the others to it. She had no desire to put her feet into the icy water again, preferring to climb the steep slope that would get her to the old bridge by way of the forest road.

Bernadette and Toinette tied up their wood and took hold of it. But Bernadette was no longer the one in the rear. She got to the top first, dropped her load on the road, and came back to help a stunned Toinette.

'But I'm the stronger one!'

'What can I do for you?' replied Bernadette.

Suddenly Toinette became insistent: 'Tell me what you saw ... Just me! I promise not to talk to anyone! Not even to May!'

In a few brief words Bernadette confided the secret of the apparition to Toinette. It aroused in Toinette both fear and a certain envy of Bernadette. For she was the eldest, the 'heir', the one who was bought stockings because of her asthma and who got white bread because of her stomach.

'You want to frighten me, but I don't care now that we are back on the road.'

She hit Bernadette with a branch from her bundle.

'Silly nonsense!'

'Oh, you can believe me,' said Bernadette calmly, warding off the blows.

They made their way back to the Baous gate, the paving stones, the Gaol. François Soubirous was still in his bed. Meal time had passed, but May's first thought was to clean the sprigs out of the children's hair. She was obsessed by the threat of skin infection.

'Toinette!'

'You always start with me! Do Bernadette first!'

Bernadette was off in the passageway, eating her portion of bread. The sight enraged Toinette. As she herself put it:

Something was driving me to tell what Bernadette had said to me. So three times I went 'hmm', as if I was trying to clear my throat. My mother said: 'Why are you doing that? Are you sick?' No, I said, but I was going to tell you what Bernadette told me (LHA 2, p. 111).

Then she blurted out: 'Bernadette saw a white girl in the grotto of Massabielle.'

'*Práoube de you* ("Oh, poor me"),' exclaimed May. After the evictions, the failures, and the prison term, what misfortune lay in wait for them now? She gathered her remaining reserves of composure to question Bernadette: 'What did you see? Tell me! What did you see?'


## A taste of the stick

The words stuck in Bernadette's throat: 'Something white.' The stick used for beating the bedclothes was applied to the two sisters, but not as hard to the fragile body of Bernadette.

'You didn't see anything but a white rock. I forbid you to go back there.'

The father, still stretched on the bed, came out with a sententious remark that embodied his dream of maintaining his personal pride against all odds: 'There's never been anything that anyone could say against our family. You're not going to start something now.'

Neither the father nor the mother understood a thing. But what was going on with Bernadette?

'We must pray,' said Louise. 'Perhaps it may be the soul of some relative in purgatory,' she mused.

Jeanne Abadie entered. She was going to negotiate the sale of the bones they had gathered, for the celebrations of Shrovetide were almost upon them. Toinette gathered up the pile of bones they had been storing for this purpose. Fortune smiled on them. Letchina gave them twenty sou for the lot. Of this amount six sou was paid for the basket of bones collected that morning. It purchased a pound of bread, which the girls brought back to share in the Gaol. There was no more talk about what happened earlier in the day.

## A dream?

That evening the family prayed before the fireplace, in which the wood collected that morning was now burning. Bernadette was deeply stirred. A profound sense of peace invaded her and she began to weep. Her mother tried to question her, but what was there to say? Troubled, Louise went to the next floor to take counsel with Romaine Sajous. The two women came back and questioned Bernadette in the semi-darkness by her bed. Their conclusion was: 'It's a dream . . . an illusion. She must not go back to Massabielle again.'

**Don't go back there!**

On Friday, February 12, Bernadette felt drawn to the grotto. But that was out of the question.

'Get back to work,' replied her mother.

Bernadette obeyed. She didn't say any more about it that day or the next day. She was on the way to forgetting the whole matter, her mother hoped.

**In the confessional (February 13)**

On Saturday evening Bernadette entered the confessional in the nearby church, where Father Pomian was hearing the regular weekly confessions. Opening the grill in the semi-darkness, he was met with a strange admission in *patois*: 'I saw something white, in the shape of a lady.'

He let the child talk without manifesting any interest, astonished by the coherence of her remarks. One feature in particular struck him: '*Coumo u cop de bén* ("like a gust of wind").' He suddenly thought of the 'gust of wind' of Pentecost, as reported in Chapter 2 of the *Acts of the Apostles*. Where did this child get such a conviction? Where did she pick up these words, which were really beyond her?

Nevertheless Father Pomian did not attach any real importance to her disclosure. A thought came to him, which he later described as an 'impulse from God'. He said to Bernadette: 'May I speak to Reverend Father (Dean Peyramale) about this?' Bernadette said yes, astonished by the priest's deference to her. That very evening Father Pomian met Dean Peyramale on the Argelès road and informed him of this minor matter. 'We must wait and see,' was all that the Dean had to say. And he moved on to talk of other matters.

**Holy water and a big stone (February 14)**

However, the report had spread among the pupils in the 'poor children's class' at the hospice school run by the nuns. Toinette and Jeanne had talked. At the end of High Mass on Sunday (February 14) a scheme took shape in the minds of the little girls in patched dresses. Feeling a mixture of enticement and fear, they determined to go and see what Bernadette saw.

Louise gave a flat 'no', then sent them off to see their father, who was working on the common field. He was taking care of the horses from the stable of Jean-Marie Cazenave, known as Ganço, who ran the stage-coach line to Bagnères.

'No,' replied François Soubirous curtly, and went on with his work.

But the little girls found an ally in his boss. 'A lady with a rosary—that can't be anything bad,' said Ganço.

François gave in, but with certain reservations: 'I'll only give you a quarter of an hour.'

'Oh, of course, we'll be back for Vespers.'

Back at the Gaol Louise had another objection: 'What if it's something bad there!'

'We are going to take some holy water.'

The children followed the route of February 11 as far as the Pont Vieux. But instead of entering the island by way of the mill, they went up the forest road. At the point where it climbs above the grotto, the children split into two groups. The smaller ones hurried ahead with Bernadette; the bigger ones tarried. They were afraid, but they pretended disdain for the babies.

Bernadette descended the steep, slippery slope like a shot. The others found her there on her knees, but not out of breath.

'How fast you ran!'

Bernadette was not listening. She had taken out her rosary and was kneeling in prayer. The others stood around her. At the second decade of the rosary Bernadette's face changed.

'*Guérat-la!* ("There she is") ... her rosary on her arm ... She is looking at you ...!'

Bernadette's companions saw nothing. Bernadette took the vial of holy water handed to her by Marie Hilo. She sprinkled vigorously in the direction of the apparition, adjuring her 'to stay if she came from God, to go away if not'.

'But the more I sprinkled, the more she smiled; and I kept sprinkling until the bottle was empty.'

Bernadette had grown pale. She did not seem to see or hear her companions. Standing at the bottom of this gully, in a cul-de-sac with the channel behind them and the mysterious craggy rock in front of them, they felt their uneasiness growing. But Bernadette seemed happy, and the sight of her inspired peace.

Suddenly something came hurtling down the rocky cliff. It seemed to shatter on the pebbles, quite close to Bernadette, and bounced into the Gave. There were splashes here and there in the water. Panic took hold of them. Toinette, Pauline and Marie fled, shrieking loudly. They thought they were being pursued. On the opposite bank a passerby heard them shouting: 'It's following us!'

The more courageous ones did not want to abandon Bernadette. They tried to drag her away. But Bernadette did not seem to hear a word. She resisted their efforts; and she seemed unbelievably heavy.

On top of the cliff Jeanne Abadie also gave way to panic at this point, for she was responsible for the alarm and the shrieking below. To assuage her own fears she had had the idea of creating a little fright herself by balancing a stone, 'as big as a hat,' on top of the cliff. It had tumbled down into the midst of the group below.

The strength of Nicolau, the operator of the Savy mill on the canal, was needed to budge Bernadette. Able to toss sacks of flour around expertly, he was astonished at the inertia of this little girl. She was so small, yet so heavy. Her paleness and her smiles made a deep impression on him. Was she really that heavy, or was he simply losing his strength? All along the way she seemed to see something.

Her eyes were 'fastened above'.

'I put my hand over her eyes and tried to get her to bend her head, but she would raise her head again and reopen her eyes with a smile' (H 2, p. 269).

Nicolau managed to get her to his mill with great difficulty. The girls who ran away had got back home. Rumour grew in Lourdes. Some people hastened to the Savy mill; they included Louise, stick in hand. This was definitely the end. Bernadette would never go to that grotto again!

### Extravaganzas?

When Bernadette went to school the next day, Shrove Monday, she was greeted with this rebuke from the Superior, Mother Ursule Fardes: 'Have you finished with your carnival extravaganzas?'

As Bernadette left school that day, Sophie Pailhaisson was waiting for her. Sophie was a disagreeable woman in her forties. She had asked Sister Anastasie, the sternest of all the teachers and detested by the children, to point out to her the chit of a girl who was putting on 'comedies' in the grotto. Sophie was a strict moralist at heart and she wanted to give the culprit a lesson.

'Look, there she is, the brat,' said Sister Anastasie.

A hard slap landed on Bernadette's cheek.

'You rascal, you! If you go back there again, you'll be locked up' (H 2, p. 291).

Bernadette, her cheek burning, made every effort to obey and to forget—without success.

During sewing workshop that afternoon, her companions brought her over to nice Sister Damien Calmels.

'Tell Sister what you saw.'

Bernadette tried to avoid the matter and escape: 'I don't know how to speak French.'

But it was too late. The others told the story in their own way. Now and then Bernadette interrupted fiercely to correct them on some point. No, there was no bouquet! No, the apparition did not pursue them! Sister Damien was perplexed. The excited talk turns to jibes about the 'pig' grotto and the lady with bare feet. Bernadette was to hear such jibes often in the days that followed.

She now regretted that she did not follow her first impulse and keep the whole matter to herself. So she wrapped herself in the silence that had become a source of strength to her in the fields of Bartrès.

### Is it the soul of Élisa?

On Shrove Tuesday, February 16, Madame Milhet's interest in the grotto affair was aroused. She was an opulent woman in her fifties who came into a nice fortune when she married her former employer. Her seamstress, Antoinette Peyret, the bailiff's daughter, had told her about the grotto and the 'young girl' who had appeared. Wouldn't that be Élisa Latapie?

The saintly death of that 'Child of Mary', who had died on October 2 of the previous year, had made a deep impression on the people of Lourdes. Dean Peyramale had written a long letter about it to Bishop Laurence to 'console his episcopal heart'. A few hours before breathing her last, Élisa had asked to be dressed for her burial. She was to be buried in a plain dress, with her insignia as a member of the Children of Mary, but without any ribbon or lace. Now there was talk of an apparition in a white dress with a blue waist band and with a rosary on her arm. Wasn't that Élisa?

'We must clear up that point,' concluded Madame Milhet.

As one who employed Louise Soubirous from time to time, Madame Milhet entered the Gaol triumphantly and left the same way. Tomorrow, before daylight, she would take Bernadette to the grotto.

## Pen and paper (Thursday, February 18)

At 5:00 a.m. the next day, Madame Milhet was knocking at the door of the Gaol with Antoinette by her side. Bernadette was still in bed. She hurried to get ready. All three attended the first Mass of the day. Then, in the dark, they travelled down to the Pont Vieux and headed off on the forest road. Antoinette was carrying the pen and inkstand of her father, the bailiff. The first two apparitions had made it clear that one could not rely on Bernadette's simplicity. They would have to get the visitor to write her own name.

Bernadette was the first to get to the grotto. Madame Milhet arrived last, sliding down 'on the seat of her dress'. They had barely begun their rosary when Bernadette murmured: '*Qué-y-ey* ("She is here").'

When the rosary was finished, Antoinette handed the inkstand to Bernadette. The visionary advanced under the arch of the grotto and stopped beneath an inner crevice which communicated with the niche. Then she held out the bailiff's writing utensils. It had been agreed that Bernadette was to pose a question to the apparition: 'Would you be so kind as to write down your name?'

The apparition approached Bernadette, 'gliding through the opening,' as Bernadette would describe it later. But nothing was written on the paper.

The other two women were growing impatient. They saw nothing and they could not even hear Bernadette's voice. They became insistent, but Bernadette made a sign suggesting that they should keep quiet or perhaps get out of the way.

As the apparition faded they broke in on Bernadette: 'But why didn't you ask her to write down her name?'

Bernadette was astonished: 'But I certainly *did* ask!'

How is it that she was not heard? The mysterious young lady of the rock, whom Bernadette called *Aquerò* ('that' thing out of prudence and respect, heard well enough. She replied simply: *N'ey pas necessári* ("It is not necessary").'

She had her own request to make to Bernadette, and she made it in *patois*: 'Would you have the graciousness to come here for fifteen days?'

'*Aoué éra grácia*' is a polite formula of request, and Bernadette was amazed that the apparition should address a child like herself in that courteous fashion. This was the first time that she had heard her 'sweet and delicate' voice.

Bernadette had promised to come on the spur of the moment, without ever reflecting on the consequences. And she had not recognized Élisa.

'And what if it was the Holy Virgin?' remarked Madame Milhet on the way back home. Her suggestion was swallowed up by the surrounding silence.

*Madame Milhet (1813–92)*

# 3

# THE FIFTEEN DAYS OF APPARITIONS (FEBRUARY 18—MARCH 4, 1858)

**Trips in secret**

Since Bernadette had promised and since nothing had been cleared up, they must go back to the grotto! On their return to town, Madame Milhet took charge of the whole affair. She arranged for Bernadette to board at her house. That way she could take Bernadette to the grotto in secret, without a lot of coming and going between the two homes. But now Louise wanted to go along, and so did Aunt Bernarde. Through the help of reports and rumours there were eight people at the grotto on Friday, February 19; 30 people on Saturday, February 20; and 100 on Sunday, February 21.

The apparition returned, in silence. The report spread, supported by the fervour of those who were praying the rosary in the grotto. They shared the joy of Bernadette in her ecstasy, though the little visionary said nothing more.

Two questions raised the atmosphere of suspense among these simple folk: Who is it? And what will take place on the last of the fifteen days that Bernadette is to go to the grotto? Will there be some miracle, some revelation, or some disaster? Rumours ran rife.

**A police interrogation**

In the afternoon of Sunday, February 21, the little girls

of the poor children's class at the hospice school came flying out of Vespers like a flock of sparrows. Callet, the rural constable, was posted on the left side of the portal. Alongside him was another gentleman, by his outfit, of the middle-classes. But the gentleman was more alert and not as stiff as the ordinary members of the town's bourgeoisie. Callet pointed to Bernadette with his index finger: 'There she is!'

The gentleman took hold of her hood and said: '*Qu'em bas segui?* Will you follow me?' It was Police Commissioner Jacomet, with whom Bernadette's father had had dealings when the flour was stolen.

Cries of sympathy went up for the little girl: 'Poor Bernadette! They are going to put you in prison.'

She was heard to reply: 'I'm not afraid. If they put me in prison, they will let me out again.'

As yet there was no police station in Lourdes. The commissioner headed for the place where he lived, the Cénac house, which he shared with two other men: Jean-Baptiste Estrade, the excise-tax officer, and Father Pène, an assistant curate. The house was only fifty metres away, directly across from the apse of the church. People followed them and the crowd of curious onlookers grew.

Jacomet was calm. On the threshold he turned around and stopped those who were trying to enter the house. The group included members of Bernadette's family, who had been pushed to the forefront by the crowd.

'There's nothing for you to see here!'

The door closed behind the crowd and the police commissioner settled down in his office. Bernadette's first interrogation began. Behind her there was a discreet witness, Jean-Baptiste Estrade. He was soon joined by his sister, Emmanuélite, with the permission of the commissioner.

When Estrade arrived, Jacomet began his interrogation in a neutral, indifferent, cursory tone—as always.

'Your name?'

'Bernadette.'

'Bernadette what?'

She hesitated. In her neighbourhood she was called Bernadette Boly, after the place of her birth. Was that the name she should give him? Or perhaps he wanted. . . .

'Soubirous!'

'Your father?'

'François.'

'Your mother?'

'Louise.'

'Louise what?'

'Soubirous.'

'No, her maiden name.'

Bernadette hesitated a moment, then responded with the eagerness of a student who has found the right answer:

'Castérot!'

Jacomet nodded approvingly, encouraging her good will.

'Your age?'

'13 or 14.'

'Is it 13 or 14?'

'I don't know.'

'Can you read and write?'

'No, sir.'

'Have you made your First Communion?'

'No, sir.'

Jacomet was relaxed as he took down his notes. He had already gauged the child. She was simple and sincere. So who was behind her? Who was making her go to the grotto? Who had given her the idea that she had seen the Holy Virgin? For the hypothesis about some soul in purgatory had fallen by the wayside, despite all the hubbub surrounding the death of Élisa Latapie. The current prevailing idea was the one that came to Madame Milhet as she returned from the grotto on February 18: 'And what if it was the Holy Virgin?'

That was what rumour had latched on to, and that was what had reached the ears of the commissioner. He got right down to the heart of the matter. To encourage Bernadette to talk, he appeared to be admiring her.

'So then, Bernadette, you see the Holy Virgin?'

'I do not say that I have seen the Holy Virgin.'

Had he misunderstood the matter? Was the child not implicated in any plot or charge?

'Ah, good! You haven't seen anything!'

'Yes, I did see *something*!'

'Well, what did you see?'

'Something white.'

Jacomet was getting more and more disconcerted.

'Some thing or some one?'

'That thing (*Aquerò*) has the form of a little young lady (*damisèle*).'

The dialogue between Jacomet and Bernadette was in the local *patois*, the only language that Bernadette knew. Bernadette regarded the apparition as a person and said that it resembled a 'little girl' or a young girl. Nevertheless, as the commissioner noted down very hesitantly, Bernadette employed neuter, rather than masculine or feminine words, to describe the apparition. In particular, she used the word *Aquerò* (the accent is on the last syllable. In the Lourdes dialect the word means 'that thing'—neuter). On her lips the word expressed peasant prudence in the face of something unfamiliar, but also reverence in the face of an ineffable reality that was beyond her. After all, how was she to say anything about it without other people making derogatory or derisive remarks? That had been her problem since the day of the very first apparition.

Jacomet, who always understood things immediately, was having a hard time putting the picture together. He made her go back over it.

'You say *Aquerò*, that thing. . . . And that thing did not say to you: "I am the Holy Virgin"?'

'*Aquerò* did not say that to me.'

'But that is what people in the town are saying.'

Yes, that is what people were saying. Indeed that is what was being printed in the local weekly, *Le Lavedan*, at that very moment. It always came out three or four days late, and thus the February 18 issue would only hit the streets tomorrow, February 22. But Jacomet had had his eyes open and he knew that it would contain an unsigned article by Bibé the lawyer. In it Bibé wrote the following, in a slightly ironic vein:

A young girl, to all appearances afflicted with catalepsy ... is attracting the attention of the populace. The topic is nothing less than the apparition of the Holy Virgin. ...

Jacomet tried to get back on the track. He went back over the whole affair from the beginning: the handful of bones; the crossing of the canal; the branches of the wild rosebush moving (*u sarrot de brancos que anaouen*, said Bernadette); the noise *like* a gust of wind (*coumo u cop de bén*); and the appearance of *Aquerò*.

'There were other girls with you when you saw (it)?'

'Yes, sir.'

Did they see (it)?'

'No, sir.'

'How do you know?'

'They told me so.'

'Why didn't they see (it)?'

'I don't know.'

Jacomet was still careful not to contradict Bernadette. He wanted her to trust him completely and unburden everything. Then the flaw would show up of its own accord.

'Well, then, this girl, this young lady, how was she dressed?'

'A white dress, tied with a blue ribbon, a white veil on her head, and a yellow rose on each foot ... the colour of the chain of her rosary. ...'

'She had feet?'

'Her dress and the roses hid them, except for her toes.'

'Did she have hair?'

'You saw a little (*drin*) here.'

Bernadette put her fingers on her temple and traced two symmetrical lines.

'She was pretty (*bèro*)?'

'Oh yes, sir, very beautiful (*beroye*).'

'Pretty like who? Like Madame Pailhasson? Like Mademoiselle Dufo?'

The commissioner appreciated the local beauties. Indeed he was an expert on the matter. Bernadette replied with a trace of pity:

'They cannot compare with her (*N'y poden pas hè*).'

'How old was she?'

'. . . young.'

The police commissioner went on writing. Now he took down information on all the people mixed up with this apparition. His attention was drawn in particular to the involvement of Madame Milhet. She had nothing to do and she was a shrewd woman. She was smart enough to make her fortune by marrying her last employer. There was a clue worth exploring.

'Is it this woman who tells you what you are to do?'

'No.'

'But you are lodging with her!'

'No, I have returned to my own house.'

'Since when?'

'Yesterday.'

'Why?'

'My aunt did not want me to go back to her house.'

'Has Madame Milhet given you a lot of money?'

'No money.'

'Are you quite sure?'

'Yes, sir, quite sure.'

'What about the Sisters? Have you talked to the Sisters about it?'

'Yes, to Mother Superior and to the Sister in charge of the workshop.'

'And what did they tell you?'

'You mustn't bother about that. . . . You dreamed it.'

They are women of good sense, thought Jacomet. He used the support of these religious authorities to shake Bernadette's assurance.

'Yes indeed, that's right, girl. You've been dreaming.'

'No, I was very much awake.'

'You thought you saw something.'

'No, I even blinked my eyes.'

'A reflection deceived you!'

'But I have seen *Aquerò* several times, and it was dark. I cannot be mistaken all the time.'

'And the others? They have eyes too, you know. Why didn't they see (it)?'

'I don't know, but I'm sure I did.'

Persuasion had failed. It was time for dissuasion.

'Listen, Bernadette, everyone is laughing at you. They say that you are crazy. For your own sake, you must not go back to the grotto any more.'

'I promised to go for fifteen days.'

'You haven't made a promise to anyone because you've made a mistake about this! Now look here, you are going to be reasonable. You are going to promise me that you will not go back there any more!'

Bernadette was silent, but her dark eyes spoke a clear message: 'Since I have already promised, I cannot promise otherwise.'

The atmosphere of the meeting altered. The police commissioner re-read what he had written down in a tone that was not at all favourable. He deliberately changed some of Bernadette's responses.

'The Virgin smiles at me,' was written in his rough draft.

'I didn't say "the Virgin",' said Bernadette, by way of correction.

Jacomet was caught in an embarrassing situation. Since Bernadette rejected all his identification of the apparition, and even argued when he said 'the girl' or 'the young lady,' he was forced to write *Aquerò*. And when he referred to it, he didn't know whether to use the masculine pronoun *il* or the feminine *elle* with the neuter word. Yet Bernadette did talk about the apparition as if it were a person! He re-read several passages more than once, changing the order or content to test Bernadette. After reacting vigorously to his first few tricks, she lost all interest in the game.

'Sir, you have altered everything on me.'

Periods of long silence, during which Jacomet was writing, alternated with renewed barrages of questions and intimidation. Jacomet's intelligence and his profession were on trial. But no potential line of inquiry led anywhere. It was not a put-up job: by whom and why? It was not trickery: the girl was sincere. It was not the result of a desire to attract attention to herself: she was modest. It was not a confidence game: there was no money involved. Nor was it catalepsy: Bernadette was sane and not a bit overexcited. He could not get a hold on her. Jacomet felt he was at the end of his resources, but he was not one to let anybody slip through his fingers.

He began his interrogation again, this time challenging Bernadette's responses.

'That is not what you told me the first time.'

'Yes it is!'

'No!'

Jacomet had donned his official cap. It gave him a military air. The pompon on it was shaking. The tension mounted. Bernadette remained unshakable. Jacomet was growing more and more incensed, and his voice grew louder. Callet, his ear close to the door of the adjoining room, where Madame Jacomet was also listening, heard the police commissioner shouting.

'Drunken sot, brazen hussy, little whore! You are getting everyone to run after you. You want to become a little wh . . .!'

'I don't tell anyone to go there.'

'Oh sure, you are quite content to show yourself off.'

'No, I'm tired of it all.'

These last words gave the commissioner a terrible idea. He started to write feverishly at the bottom of the third page of his official stationery. His handwriting grew bigger on the fourth page; it became twice as large as it had been. He had latched on to two things which Bernadette had said: her final remark about being tired of it all, and an earlier one to the effect that she felt an inner compulsion to go to the grotto. He would use them to formulate a kind of confession: a confession that someone was forcing her to go to the grotto. Rather than 'someone', however, it would be better to put down her 'parents'. They were responsible legally and they had every reason for wishing not to attract the attention of the police again. (But let me note right here that Jacomet was honest enough to eliminate this false confession when he re-copied his rough draft after Bernadette left.)

While Jacomet's goose-quill was jotting down the last lines of his rough draft, the noise grew outside, where a large crowd had gathered. People were banging on the door and the shutters; voices were raised. Jacomet grasped the meaning of the noise and confusion. The crowd had pushed Bernadette's parents forward, for they actually had the right to be present at the interrogation. Jacomet had finished writing. Before confronting his challengers, Jacomet made one last effort with the girl he had been interrogating:

'Listen, Bernadette, you have put yourself in a bad spot. I am quite willing to fix things up between us, but on one condition. Admit that you haven't seen anything.'

'Sir, I did see something. I cannot say otherwise.'

'At least promise me that you will not go back to the grotto any more. This is your last chance.'

'Sir, I promised to go there.'

'All right, have it your way. I am going to get the policemen to take you to prison.'

Jacomet got up. Bernadette did not budge. In actual fact Jacomet headed for the front door, where someone was knocking for him. The crowd had pushed François Soubirous to the forefront.

'They don't have the right to interrogate her without you!'

'Go on in, if you love your daughter!'

François, too, was getting angry. He did indeed love his daughter. He would not have anyone saying that he did not know how to defend her.

Suddenly the door opened. François found himself face-to-face with the police commissioner. He entered, full of spirit. But the door was quickly closed behind him, and he suddenly found himself alone with the police commissioner. From all the experience of his humble life, he knew that innocence is not enough to keep a person out of prison. He had taken off his beret and was fingering it, not knowing what to do next. He made his claim humbly and politely.

'I am the father of the little one.'

Jacomet became his most amiable:

'Ah good, Father Soubirous, I am pleased to see you. I was just on the point of sending for you, because this comedy cannot go on any longer. You are attracting people to your house.'

'But. . . .'

'I know everything now. The little girl is tired of the whole thing, she told me. She has had enough of you people forcing her to go down there.'

'Forcing her? We have done everything to stop her!'

'But that is what she ended up telling me in tears, and here it is written down on this paper by me: "Papa and mama are outside. You must prohibit them from forcing me to go to the grotto. I'm tired of it all, and I don't want to go there any more".'

François looked anxiously at the piece of paper, akin to the one that got him sent to prison less than a year ago, but he could not read a single treacherous word of it. Bernadette was protesting vigorously, but the commissioner kept her out of it. Now it was between him and her father.

'Good, good, Father Soubirous! I myself would like to believe you, but it's up to you to prove you are sincere. Forbid Bernadette to return to the grotto and shelter her from all the people who are running after her. Then the whole affair will be over.'

François Soubirous was conciliatory.

'It is true that we are weary of seeing our home invaded, and that we've done everything to prevent her from going to that place. In giving me this order, you're doing me a service. I'll close my door to people, and the little one won't go to the grotto any more.'

François left, content to have recovered his daughter.

And Jacomet was happy to have landed on his feet once again.

Bernadette left as she had entered, not a bit shaken or beaten. The police commissioner who made such an impression on everyone had not intimidated her a bit. Now she couldn't help but smile over his feints, his accusations, and his fits of anger. When Dominique Cazenave questioned her about the interrogation and the commissioner back at the Gaol, Bernadette replied with a laugh:

'He was trembling. And there was a tassel on his cap which kept going ting-a-ling.'

## No appearance (Monday, February 22)

The next day Bernadette was again confronted with her own problems. In the morning she felt a strong urge to go to the grotto. The answer was 'no'. Bernadette tried to obey as usual. But she felt ill at ease because she had promised to go to the grotto for fifteen days. No reasoning reassured her. She replied: 'Then I must disobey either you or *Aquerò*.'

Bernadette was under great stress, and struggling within herself. Mother Superior, who had seen her led away by the police commissioner the previous afternoon, congratulated her on the end of her 'carnival extravaganzas'. The jibes of her companions continued. But all that was nothing compared to the inner laceration Bernadette felt. Never had obedience weighed so heavy on her as it did this interminable morning.

Bernadette was on her way back to school after her meagre midday meal. But as she passed the threshold of the colonnade, an inner force brought her back to herself. She pivoted on the spot and started for Massabielle by the quickest possible route. She went down through the mill quarter of her childhood and turned left on the Pè de Pesquè path, between the castle-fortress and the Gave. She was being followed by others; not only by sympathizers but also by policemen who were watching her return to school. Bernadette was not at ease; her disobedience disturbed her. At the Pont Vieux she stopped. She had no candle as she did at other times. Aunt Bernarde sent someone to fetch one from Aunt Lucile's.

Now Sergeant D'Angla arrived on the heels of the policemen. He shrugged his shoulders on seeing the gathering that had been so quickly improvised:

'Here in the nineteenth century they would like to have us believe in this sort of superstition!'

Bernadette was in her usual place in front of the rock, but this time she was flanked by Sergeant D'Angla. He kept repeating the same thing, growing more and more ironic as he went along:

'Do you see her? . . . Do you see her? . . . You see her as much as I do!'

Bernadette was silent. To those who were in the grotto the preceding days it was clear that nothing had taken place. Bernadette finished her rosary without any change in her countenance. No light had come to pierce the darkness, and her distress aroused the bystanders' sympathy. Aunt Bernarde put out the candle and led her off to rest at the Savy mill, as she had done on February 14.

Sergeant D'Angla was triumphant: 'The wings of my cap sent the apparition flying off!' The comments of the people varied, 'It's a lot of foolishness,' said some. 'It's because of the policemen,' said others. 'The hour had passed,' said still others. The last explanation was the one accepted by the 'believers', as they were now beginning to be called.

Bernadette herself murmured: 'I don't know in what way I have failed her. . . .'

That evening she slipped into Father Pomain's confessional for the second time. She posed her problem of conscience to him. Prompted by some inexplicable inner impulse, he settled the matter conscientiously: 'They do not have the right to stop you.'

At the very same moment the authorities were deliberating about the same matter. A conference was being held by Sergeant D'Angla, Prosecutor Dutour, and Mayor Lacadé. The latter made this observation:

> The prohibition has no legal basis. Public opinion is on the side of the little girl, and they will not fail to blame us if we take action against her. She must be kept under surveillance, to be sure, but it would be a mistake to repress her.

This moderate opinion prevailed. Bernadette's knotty situation was untangled.

### The seventh apparition (Tuesday, February 23)

On February 23, Bernadette was on her way to the grotto by 5:30 a.m. The number of people at the grotto was around 150, almost a crowd. For the first time one could see there, not only the berets and hoods of the poorer people, but also the fancy hats of society ladies and gentlemen. Even some of the intelligentsia who met at the *Café français* were present: Doctor Dozous; Monsieur Dufo, a lawyer and town councillor; and Jean-Baptiste Estrade, who had been present at the police commissioner's interrogation of Bernadette two days before. Estrade was secretly interested in the matter, but he was also perplexed. He was present today only because of the insistent pleading of his sister Emmanuélite and her friends, whose curiosity had reached fever pitch. Estrade himself had come only to serve as a knightly escort, for young ladies from good families did not go out by themselves in this era. He was sceptical and ironic on the trip to the grotto, a convinced enthusiast on the way back home afterwards. Bernadette's ecstasy captivated him completely:

> I saw Mademoiselle Rachel in the Bordeaux theatre. She is magnificent ... but infinitely inferior to Ber-

nadette. . . . That child has a supernatural being in front of her.

Estrade's 'conversion' spread the news and the credibility of the apparition. But *Aquerò* still maintained her silence and Bernadette still did not know her name.

## The eighth apparition (Wednesday, February 24)

On Wednesday, February 24, Bernadette had a hard time getting to 'her' place amid a crowd of almost 300 people. After her recitation of the rosary in ecstasy, something new was added. Bernadette advanced a couple of paces on her knees, and then she seemed to throw her face on the ground.

Her Aunt Lucile, aged eighteen, was at her side. When Bernadette did this, Lucile let out a cry and fainted. Bernadette was startled. She had just prostrated herself and kissed the ground at the request of the apparition.

Bernadette returned to reality around her to say: 'Auntie, don't be troubled.' But the apparition was gone. Today she had uttered a new word and repeated it: 'Penitence!' She said: 'Pray to God for the conversion of sinners.' Then she had asked Bernadette to perform a penitential exercise: 'Go and kiss the ground as a penance for sinners.' That was the gesture performed by Bernadette which had such an impact on Aunt Lucile.

## Muddy water (Thursday, February 25)

On February 25, people began to flock to the grotto around 2:00 a.m. For there were not too many spots where one could get a good view of what was going on. All night people were knocking on partitions and shutters, alerting their friends. When the visionary arrived at the grotto, there were 350 people there.

Bernadette recited the rosary in ecstasy as usual. Then, after handing her candle and her white hood to Éléonore Pérard beside her, she repeated the action that had been interrupted by Aunt Lucile the day before. On her knees she crawled up the sloping ground that led to the back of the grotto. Now and then she kissed the ground. Her effortless agility on the pebbly ground was surprising. People made room for her. They were watching to see what would happen.

Bernadette arrived beneath the open crevice of the vault, a vertical chimney that communicated with the niche where the apparition was. Bernadette stopped. Her lips were moving. But as is always the case in these conversations that open out on another world, no one could hear the sound of her voice. Bernadette seemed to give her assent. Then suddenly she was coming back out, still on her knees, and moving towards the Gave. There something brought her to a halt. She went back towards the niche and headed in the opposite direction towards the very back of the grotto, standing this time. At the point where the bottom of the vault joined the sloping moraine floor Bernadette bent down. Her eyes seemed to be searching for something or other. Disturbed, she came back out again, loked once more at the inner cavity, and then went back in. This time she bent down to the ground, reluctantly regarded the muddy soil saturated with water, cast an embarrassed glance at the cavity, scraped the soil with her right hand to form a little hole. She then drew a kind of reddish mud out of the hole, brought it to her face, rejected it with disgust, and began again. She would have really liked to drink this filthy water, but her repugnance was too great. She managed to do it only on the fourth try. Then she ate a few of the round-leafed herbs growing at the back of the grotto: golden saxifrage (D 4, pp. 391–393).

What in heaven's name was she doing? The onlookers didn't understand a thing. When she came back out, her face all dirty, there was consternation.

'She's nuts!' some whispered.

Estrade's enthusiasm had drawn some of his friends to the grotto with him. They wanted to see this rival of the famous Rachel (who had died the preceding month). Now they did not conceal their disappointment. Elfrida Lacrampe, the daughter of the innkeeper, exploded with the language of her father's grooms when she got angry. She was angry now: 'As far as Rachel is concerned, you've brought us out to see a little craphead!'

Estrade did not know what to say. His fervour had collapsed. He admitted his plight: 'I am completely at a loss. I don't understand it at all.' There would be plenty of debate that evening at the *Café français*, and he would cut a very poor figure.

To those who asked her about it, Bernadette offered this explanation:

*Aquerò* told me:
'Go and drink at the spring and wash yourself in it.' Not seeing any water, I went to the Gave. But she indicated with her finger that I should go under the rock. I found a little water, more like mud: so little that I could scarcely cup it in my hand. Three times I threw it away, it was so dirty. On the fourth try I managed to drink it.

'But why did she ask you to do that?'

'She didn't tell me.'

'What about the herb that you ate?'

Bernadette had no reply.

'D'you know that people think you're crazy to do things like that?'

'For sinners,' was Bernadette's only reply, repeating what she had heard while she was in her state of ecstasy.

Sinners and sin: was it such a serious matter as all that? The look and tone of Bernadette opened new horizons.

In the afternoon some of the people returned to the grotto. They looked at the hole that Bernadette had dug. It was as 'big as a soup-tureen'. Éléonore Pérard planted a stick in the basin of muddy water and detected the gurgle of flowing water. Others tried to take a drink as Bernadette had done. The more they dug out the hole and drew off water, the more the water spouted up and the clearer it became. A patch of mud that was turning into pure water: one began to grasp the message demanding the conversion of sinners.

Two bottles of the water went back to town that day. Jeanne Montat took one to her sick father. 'He must drink some of this water,' she thought to herself.

The other bottle was brought back by the son of the tobacconist, who wore a patch over his eye. In the days that followed, Jacquette Pène, the sister of the assistant curate (Father Pène), observed that the boy was no longer wearing the patch. She had seen him drawing water from the hole.

### A session with the Imperial Prosecutor

That same evening a police agent appeared at the Gaol: 'The Imperial Prosecutor requests Bernadette Soubirous to present herself at his home this evening at 6:00 p.m.'

François Soubirous was at the big market in Tarbes, to which he had driven one of Cazenave's coaches. What was Louise to do? In tears she appealed to Cousin Sajous, who was working at the Ger quarry. He hurried home and donned his Sunday suit.

The prosecutor lived 300 metres away in the Claverie house, on the Rue Marcadalouse. (Today that house is the rectory of Lourdes, and the name of the street has been changed to Rue de Bagnères.) When they got there, the prosecutor cast a suspicious glance at the fellow accompanying the two females.

'Are you her father?'

'No, her uncle, and the master of the house where she stays.'

'Bernadette, you and your mother come in. You, wait here!'

Sajous was blocked from entering and the door was closed on him.

The interrogation was conducted according to the rules, as was that of the police, but the pace was not as brisk. Prosecutor Dutour was a meticulous intellectual. He did not have Jacomet's feline resourcefulness. He sought to impress the culprit by taking refuge behind his office and his timidity. But neither the trappings of justice nor the solemnity of the inkstand intimidated Bernadette.

The prosecutor started off well enough. He was aloof, methodical, authoritative. But Bernadette's answers upset his plans and he lost the thread of his argument. It was the one fault of this irreproachable man, pitilessly noted in the reports of his superiors and evident in his own drafts. Bernadette laughed when she saw him missing the hole in his inkstand. He had exhausted every means to uncover fabrication, over-excitement, self-interest, and the other classic motives. He tried to finish the business.

'You are going to promise me not to go back to the grotto any more.'

'I promised to go there for fifteen days.'

'A promise made to a lady that no one sees isn't worth anything. You must stay away.'

'I feel a great deal of joy when I go there.'

'Joy is a bad counsellor. Listen instead to the Sisters, who told you that it was an illusion.'

'I am drawn there by an irresistible force.'

'And what if you are put in prison, what will you do then?'

'Oh, if I can't go, then I won't.

Monsieur Dutour made a last attempt at intimidation.

'Go and tell the commissioner to come for the little girl and have her put in prison.'

May suddenly burst out sobbing. She had been standing alongside Bernadette for two hours, and now she was tottering. Bernadette was standing too. The prosecutor took notice.

'There are chairs. You can sit down.'

His tone suggested the condescension and disdain that

would show up in his next report. Bernadette sensed the undertones and blurted out immediately:

'No, I would soil it.'

So while May flopped into a chair pushed over to her by Madame Dutour, Bernadette sat herself 'on the ground like tailors do'.

People were now banging on the shutters. Sajous and his friends, who had had time to down a few drinks in his cousin's café across the way, were beginning to make a scene. The prosecutor began to tremble. His hand could not find the hole of his inkstand.

After a few final words of intimidation, the two women were released. The interrogation had not been a success. Later the prosecutor would destroy the disordered notes of his draft. Meanwhile Bernadette and her mother were taken across the street for a final drink at Sajous' café.

It was almost nine o'clock when Bernadette got back home to the Gaol. Dominiquette Cazenave eyed her when she entered.

'So, did you confess?'

'Yes, I told the truth. They speak lies.'

She simply could not understand the tricks and contradictions of those gentlemen. She asked:

'When a person doesn't write well, does he make crosses? The prosecutor kept making crosses (i.e., scratching out things on his notes).' Bernadette laughed.

'What a child you are!' exclaimed her mother.

Bernadette's account was to be inflated to fantastic proportions by the populace. The trembling of the prosecutor became St Vitus' dance. His crossings out became big crosses that he felt compelled to put down on his paper. And that evening, people would assure their listeners, the candles in his house lit up by themselves. Bernadette would have nothing to do with this mythology.


**No apparition (February 26)**

On the morning of February 26 she found herself again in

the same situation she had been in on February 22 after her interrogation by the police commissioner. She was forbidden to go to the grotto. The prohibition came from higher up. But today a group of people were waiting at her door. Bernarde Castérot, conscious of her duties as the eldest, had come to the Gaol. She was sitting on the table, perplexed. Bernadette looked at the family authority and waited for her to say something.

'If I were in Bernadette's place, I would go!'

Without a word Bernadette took down her white hood from the wall.

Today there were almost 600 people at the grotto. It took an immense amount of good will on the part of everyone to get Bernadette to 'her' place. She recited the rosary. Nothing happened. She again performed her penitential exercise for sinners. Nothing happened. She made a gesture of supplication. Those close to her who were watching this interpreted for the others:

'Everyone, on your knees!'

But *Aquerò* had requested nothing. *Aquerò* was not there. Bernadette washed herself in the spring, which had grown clearer during the night. She prayed in vain. They took her to the Savy mill, her refuge on unhappy days. Inconsolable, she asked herself:

'What have I done to her?'

### The penitential apparitions (February 27–March 1)

*Aquerò* was there to meet Bernadette the next morning, February 27. The crowd was larger, despite the disappointments of the two preceding days. One of the new arrivals was Antoine Clarens, headmaster of the high school in Lourdes. He had come to shed the light of his education on this murky affair.

When Clarens got back home, he started to prepare a memorandum entitled *La grotte de Lourdes*. It was for the prefect, his friend and patron. The exercises of the visionary, crawling on her knees and kissing the ground, made a bad impression on Clarens. That evening he went to question Bernadette. The naïve assurance of the child and her 'charm' impressed him. Without emphasis she explained the meaning of her strange acts:

'In penance, first for myself, and then for others.'

Clarens was perplexed. The light of his knowledge, so effective in dispelling popular superstition, could not come to bear on Bernadette's limpidity.

In the presence of an ever growing crowd Bernadette continued her penitential exercises the next day and the day after that. 1,150 people were present on Sunday, February 28. That same day Renault, the commandant of the constabulary forces, came from Tarbes to discuss measures made necessary by the growing crowd. For the people at the grotto were wedged in dangerously between a sheer cliff and the Gave River.

When High Mass was over, the warden of springs, Latapie, grabbed Bernadette by her hood. There would be another interrogation that day, as there had been last Sunday. This time it was conducted by Judge Clément Ribes, the examining magistrate. The judge came up against Bernadette's resolve to go to the grotto 'till Thursday,' because she had 'promised'. He was without legal means to stop her.

On Monday, March 1, people arrived at the grotto around midnight. An atmosphere of quiet and meditation prevailed. Prayer was improvised on the spot. There was a crowd of 1,500 people. One could see the white cloaks of the Visens soldiers and, at the last minute, the cassock of a priest. His name was Father Désirat, and he was not from Lourdes. He was unaware of the fact that Dean Peyramale had forbidden the clergy to go to the grotto. His arrival created a sensation and people made way for him. Much to his own bewilderment, he found himself in the front row. His eyes bulging like two saucers, he saw Bernadette in ecstasy. It left an indelible impression on him:

Her smile passes all description. Neither the most capable artist nor the most consummate actor could ever reproduce her charm and grace. Impossible to imagine it.

What struck me was the joy and the sadness on her face. When one succeeded the other, it happened with the speed of lightning. But ... there was nothing brusque about it: a marvellous transition. I had observed the child when she came to the grotto. I had watched her with meticulous attention. What a difference there was between the girl she was then and the girl I saw at the moment of the apparition!

Respect, silence, recollection reigned everywhere. Oh, how good it was there! I thought I was in the vestibule of paradise.

## The first miracle

That day there occurred at the grotto the first of the seven cures that the bishop would eventually regard as the 'work of God'. But he was to do so only after long inquiries by the episcopal commission and Professor Vergez, M.D. (D 6, p. 260; see D 5, pp. 168–69, 263–64, 357).

In the middle of the night Catherine Latapie, called Chouat, set out for Lourdes. She was nine months pregnant. She took her two youngest children with her on the trip to the grotto, which was seven kilometres away. She was acting on a sudden impulse, driven by desperation. In October 1856 she had climbed an oak tree to knock down acorns for her hogs. She had fallen from the tree. The doctor had been able to set the disabled arm, but two fingers on her right hand had remained paralysed and doubled up. It was a disaster for Catherine because she could no longer spin, or knit, or do anything useful.

She witnessed the apparition with her two little ones. Then she climbed to the back of the grotto, to the source of the little stream of water that now flowed to the Gave.

She plunged her hand into the water and felt a wave of softness flow over her. The bent fingers had suddenly regained their suppleness.

A violent labour-pain cut short her prayer of thanksgiving. She murmured: 'Holy Virgin who has just cured me, let me get back home!'

Quickly she grabbed the two children by the hand and hurried over the seven kilometres to Loubajac. When she got home, she went into labour without any help and 'almost without pain'. The midwife, alerted hastily, arrived only in time to hear the first cry of the newborn babe. It was a boy, to be named Jean-Baptiste. He would become a priest.

**A chapel and a procession (March 2)**

At the end of her ecstasy before 1,650 people on March 2, Bernadette set out for the rectory. She was preceded there by some of the devout, who had received a message from her:

'Go and tell the priests that people are to come here in procession and to build a chapel here.'

The devout listeners recalled only the first point: the procession. It was an urgent matter in their eyes. It obviously was meant for the 'big day', Thursday, the day after tomorrow which would mark the close of the fifteen days! Bernadette did not say this specifically, but it was obvious to the people.

Bernadette hurried to bring this message to the rectory, but she did not stay there long. For Dean Peyramale immediately realized the consequences of the authorization of a procession right now. The authorities were concerned with the stopping of the flow of foolish people to the grotto, the bishop in all likelihood would have refused to authorize any such project, and it would have brought down ridicule on Dean Peyramale. Irritation mounted inside him, all the more because he felt obliged to neutral-

ize his inexplicable propensity to believe who was at work
in all this, seeing as he did all the fruits of grace evident in
his parish. The devout bore the brunt of this interior
conflict. They were met with one of the sudden bursts of
anger of which the Dean was capable when he was faced
with difficult matters.

Now Bernadette arrived with her two aunts, Bernarde
and Basile. They got a poor reception.

'You're the one who goes to the grotto?'

'Yes, Reverend Father.'

'And you say that you see the Holy Virgin?'

'I did not say that it is the Holy Virgin.'

'Then who is this lady?'

'I don't know.'

'So, you don't know! Liar! Yet those you get to run after
you and the newspaper say that you claim to see the Holy
Virgin. Well, then, what do you see?'

'Something that resembles a lady.'

'Something! *Quaouqu' arré*!'

The dialect word sounded out like a clap of thunder.
Bernadette tried to convey the request for a procession.
But there was thorough confusion. She did not know that
the devout had been to the rectory ahead of her and had
asked for a procession *on Thursday*. The priest's anger
rose again. He fought against aggression and against himself. He stalked up and down the room, repeating:

'So, then! A lady! A procession!'

He regarded the two aunts, both of whom he had chased
out of the Children of Mary because they had become
pregnant before marriage ('farted at Vespers,' as the local
saying put it).

'It is unfortunate to have a family like this, which cre-
ates disorder in the town.' He cast a withering glance at
Bernadette: 'Keep her in check and don't let her budge
again.'

Aunt Bernarde had stolen away. Basile and Bernadette
shrunk to the size of two pins.

'Get out of here!'

This last remark of Dean Peyramale's sounded as if he

were saying: 'Get thee behind me, Satan!'

'You will never get me to go see Reverend Father again,' said Basile when they left. But a few steps farther on, Bernadette stopped!

'Oh, Aunt Basile, we must go back! I forgot to tell him about the chapel!'

'Don't count on me any more! Really, you're making me sick!'

Bernadette looked in vain for someone to go with her. Everyone turned their backs—except, in the end, Dominiquette Cazenave, the sister of the station-master for whom François Soubirous worked. Dominiquette went off to the rectory alone and arranged a meeting for later. It was to take place at 7:00 p.m., when Reverend Father would have calmed down.

There were several priests at the meeting: Father Pène, Father Serres, and Father Pomian, her confessor. It was a solemn assembly indeed. Bernadette conveyed the second part of her commission:

'Go and tell the priests to have a chapel built here' (H 5, p. 182).

But she was so deeply affected that, for the one and only time in her life, she added her own commentary on the message:

'A chapel ... as quickly as possible, even if it be very small.'

'A chapel? Is it as it was for the procession? Are you sure of it?'

'Yes, Reverend Father, I am sure of it.'

The shock and bustle of the morning had erased the request for a procession from the frail memory of Bernadette. Did the apparition really talk about Thursday? What words had she used? Everything had disappeared from her mind, as the catechism phrases did when she was in Bartrès. Bernadette retained a vague idea of the procession. But she could not in all honesty be precise about it.

'You still don't know what her name is?'

'No, Reverend Father.'

'Well, then, you must ask her.'

Dean Peyramale lapsed into silence. The other men present picked up the conversation, raising all the questions that had come to surround the event. Father Pomian was afraid that there would be a resurgence of folklore and local superstitions:

'Have you heard talk of fairies?'

'No, Father.'

'Have you heard talk of witches?' asked another.

'No, Father,' replied Bernadette (all of this in the local dialect, of course).

'You're lying! Everyone has heard talk of witches in Lourdes.'

Dominiquette had experience on the stage-coach line, so she had become quite an expert in unravelling misunderstandings due to dialect differences between one valley and the next. At this point she intervened:

'Father, she doesn't understand you. Talk to her about *broúches. Sourcieros* doesn't mean anything in the local dialect here.'

Father Pomian mobilized his knowledge of the local *patois* to ask his question:

'What are the *paráoulos* the lady spoke to you?'

'There is no *paráou* in there,' replied Bernadette.

'What? No words! But this chapel, this procession!'

Dominiquette interrupted again: 'Father, she does not understand you. In Lourdes people say *parólos*, not *paráoulos* as they do in your valley. When you say *paráou*, it means "kneading trough" to her.'

Then Dominiquette added: 'Reverend Father, let her go!'

Bernadette left on Dominiquette's arm, feeling buoyant.

'I am quite content. I performed my commission!'

**The vigil (March 3)**

On March 3 there were 3,000 people at the grotto. Clusters of people were clinging to every nook and cranny of the cliff and the slope. They prayed for hours, but few managed to see Bernadette. What happened that morning? Contradictory reports circulated in town. Some said she did see the apparition. Others said she did not.

The fact is that *Aquerò* did not appear among the early morning throng. Bernadette left the grotto upset, as she had on February 22 and February 26. But she came back a little later on the footpath leading to the fort. And this time *Aquerò* kept her rendezvous.

That evening, when Dean Peyramale returned from Tarbes where he went to consult with Father Ribes, Bernadette rang the doorbell of the rectory.

'Reverend Father, the lady still wants the chapel.'

'Did you ask her for her name?'

'Yes, but she only smiled.'

'She is having a lot of fun with you!'

The fervour and the conversions which the Dean knew of in the parish nurtured hope in him. He got the idea of asking for a sign that would erase his perplexity. In the sixteenth century the Virgin had appeared in Guadalupe (Mexico). There she had caused the hillside to flower in the dead of winter.

'Well, then, if she wants the chapel, let her tell you her name and cause the rosebush in the grotto to flower. Then we will have a chapel built, and it will not be "quite small" at all. No! It will be nice and big,' added Dean Peyramale, who didn't go for shabbiness.

## The big day (Thursday, March 4, 1858)

The last day of the fifteen had come. It was the 'big day', as everyone put it. At 11:00 p.m. the night before, the police commissioner was at the grotto. He inspected all its cavities to make sure that no fake machinery or fireworks had been planted to ensure a miracle. He was astonished to find people there already. And they were praying!

At 5:00 a.m. he repeated his inspection. It was difficult to do because the people were crushed into every nook and cranny of the grotto. They had come from all the surrounding valleys. By 6:00 a.m. the policemen of Argelès and Saint Pè had assembled in front of the town hall. The soldiers from the fort were there too. Some people were already on guard duty along the road.

Daybreak revealed a huge crowd massed on both banks of the Gave. The red hoods of the people from Barèges mingled with the white hoods of the people from Lourdes. The castle-fortress atop the peak, which dominates the crossroads of the seven valleys, had never looked down on so many people, particularly in this deserted spot. Estimates ranged from 8,000 to 20,000. (As usual, it is safer to go with the lower figure.)

The crowd was astonishingly calm. The praying had not ceased. People had put up with the crowding, the cramping, and even with the moving back and forth that dipped the front row into the canal waters now and then. Fortunately, it was the shallow spot where Bernadette began to take off her stockings on February 11.

At 7:00 a.m., the usual hour in recent days, Bernadette wasn't there. Anxiety mounted. The crowd was getting exasperated, aching and fatigued. Had the authorities locked Bernadette up illegally? Keenly aware of the mood of the crowd, Commissioner Jacomet, who had been on the scene since 5:00 a.m., sent young Tarbès to find out what was going on:

'Go and see if Bernadette is on her way!'

At 7:05 the crowd on the slope broke into noisy chatter: 'There she is!'

Bernadette had arrived, in the company of Jeanne Védère, her grown-up cousin. Jeanne, aged 30, was the Momères school-teacher. Bernadette had promised her that she could be by her side during this apparition. The two females attended Low Mass at 6:30 a.m. and left at the last blessing for the grotto.

The crowd found some way to move aside so that Bernadette and her entourage could pass. The agents of law and order merely assisted the good will of the whole assembly. In fact Bernadette had made her own provisions earlier. Having found her way blocked the previous day, and having missed the apparition on the first morning trip, Bernadette had decided to do something on her own. That day she had climbed the winding steps of the Rue des Espénettes to ask Ganço for assistance. He was her father's employer, he really knew how to pack people in all right when he drove the stage-coach at full speed. That evening Tarbès, the wheelwright, had erected a foot-bridge of wooden planks down at the grotto so that Bernadette could arrive on the spot at the appointed hour and thus not miss her meeting.

And now, the next day, she was right in her place! But Jeanne Védère, alas, was stopped on the far side of the foot-bridge. The crowd formed right behind the visionary. But Bernadette had not forgotten her promise and so she asked for her cousin. People hung on her every word. Jacomet and a policeman crossed the foot-bridge and pointed to Jeanne, one of the many gazing enviously at the bridge:

'Are you the one?'

In the twinkling of an eye Jeanne found herself right alongside her cousin Bernadette, as the latter had promised.

At the third Hail Mary of the second decade of the rosary, Bernadette went into ecstasy. The police commissioner and the deputy-mayor were busy taking notes in their books. Jacomet was particularly diligent in noting every gesture that Bernadette made: '34 smiles and 24 bows in the direction of the grotto.' The crowd imitated her Signs of the Cross. At the end of a half-hour, Bernadette went under the roof of the grotto to the place where she held her conversations with the apparition. Her lips moved, but no sound filtered out to the crowd around her. For two minutes she remained there, completely happy. During those two minutes alone, according to Jeanne Védère, Bernadette smiled eighteen times, grew sad for three minutes, and then brightened up again.

Afterwards Bernadette bowed, returned to her original spot, and took up the recitation of the rosary for another fifteen minutes. Then, without saying a word, she extinguished her candle and headed back towards Lourdes, paying no heed to the passionate interest of the throng. The apparition had been a long one, lasting a good three-quarters of an hour (from 7:15 to 8:00 a.m.).

However, there had been no miracle and no revelation. The crowd dwindled away, calm but perplexed. The police commissioner and the sergeant were feeling triumphant on two counts. First of all, the apparition had been a big disappointment. Secondly, the forces of law and order had done very well, avoiding any incident or accident. Those two facts, particularly the disappointment of the event, would be much discussed in the press in the days that followed.

That morning, however, a crowd of people gathered in front of the Gaol. In a queue that seemed never to end, the people wanted to see Bernadette in person, to touch or embrace her. She herself protested:

'And what will be next after that?'

It was useless to resist. She tried to hold up the queue by delaying, but that did not work. Finally, to speed up the process, she said:

'Let them all in at once. . . .' (H 5, p. 336).

To her surprise, her companion of the morning, Jeanne Védère got in the queue and came to present her rosaries to Bernadette. She had three of them: her ordinary rosary, that of the Seven Sorrows, and that of the Camaldolese.

'You too!' exclaimed Bernadette. 'What in heaven's name do you want me to do? I'm not a priest!'

With great difficulty the family managed to close the door during the midday-meal hour, when there was a lull in the crowd.

Bernadette took advantage of this moment to carry out her commission to Dean Peyramale. He was waiting for her, hopefully and not without emotion.

'What did the lady say?'

'I asked her for her name . . . She smiled. I asked her to

make the rosebush flower, and she kept smiling. But she still wants the chapel.'

'Do you have the money to build this chapel?'

'No, Reverend Father.'

'Neither do I. Tell the lady to give it to you.'

Both he and Bernadette were disappointed that the awaited answer was not given by the lady on this, the last day.

Disguising herself as best she could, Bernadette headed for 15 Rue du Bourg where Antoine Clarens lived. The headmaster had invited her to take refuge from the crowd in his own home. He was amazed to see her enter so wholeheartedly into the play of his young children. His youngest was Marie-Jeanne, aged four.

But the crowd was gathering again outside the Gaol. They had found out where she was hiding. The three doctors who saw her early that morning had held a meeting and were now demanding her return. Between 3:00 and 4:00 p.m. François Soubirous picked up his daughter and took her back to the Gaol. The queue of people continued until the evening. Bernadette was finally worn out by all the embracing and begged for relief:

'Lock the door!'

'The foul, sombre hovel,' mentioned in the prosecutor's report three days earlier had become a courtly waiting room. People wanted to meet Bernadette or to leave money and gifts. Bernadette rejected their efforts with surprising vigour:

'It burns me,' she exclaimed, when someone tried to slip a gold coin into her hand.

That was lucky for her, because traps had been laid by others. First a policeman was sent, because the officials assumed that some sort of confidence game was involved. But that dodge was a bit too obvious. Then some private citizens were employed, including the wife of Sergeant D'Angla. Bernadette, however, did not know the technique of accepting tips suavely. She rejected all the money offered her with surprising vehemence.

Why was there such excitement and enthusiasm after

the disappointment of the early morning? An event which took place on Bernadette's way from the grotto had served to rekindle people's hopes. On the slope leading up to the forest road Bernadette had suddenly slowed down and almost come to a dead stop. Gançó, who was holding her with his right hand while fending off the crowd with his left, turned around. Bernadette was looking compassionately at a little girl wearing a red hood. A native of Barèges, she had tried to approach Bernadette when she arrived at the grotto. Her name was Eugénie Troy and she was the same age as Bernadette. She was ill and she wore a bandage over her eyes because she could not tolerate light. Gançó noticed Bernadette's affectionate look.

'Let the girl from Barèges approach.'

The crowd parted for her and the two young girls embraced each other, laughing and holding hands. Bernadette embraced her a second time and then continued on her way, without having asked the girl her name. Now the girl in the red hood became the centre of everyone's attention; she had taken off her bandage to look at the visionary. The light of day, so painfully dazzling for her, no longer bothered her at all. She was carried away with joy.

'A miracle! A blind person has been healed!'

The news spread 'with the rapidity of an electric spark,' to use the new metaphor of Dean Peyramale. The crowd gathered around the girl from Barèges. She went back down to the grotto and washed in the spring. Excitement was at its peak and the crowd led her to Prosecutor Dutour. They wanted this unbeliever to corroborate the miracle, and they were scandalized by his reserve and his scepticism.

Dean Peyramale seems to have been more accepting, particularly because of the warm feeling in the account of the girl's father:

'With the utmost conviction and with tears in his eyes, he swore that his daughter recovered her sight miraculously' (Letter of Peyramale, March 9, 1858: D 1, pp. 230–231).

The people from Barèges testified in the same vein. On the spot Peyramale formulated a verbal deposition for the bishop, but with the reservation that there would be a closer enquiry. The next day, March 5, he wrote to the priest in the girl's parish. There was a delay in that priest's response because he was away. After the middle of March he did come to Lourdes himself, and his report was as disappointing as it possibly could be. The girl was never blind, but the state of her health was not good. She was very ill. Her joy over the visit to Lourdes had aroused illusions shared by her parents. There could be no talk about a cure. This verdict was confirmed by Doctor Theil, who was sent there expressly to verify the situation. Peyramale's disappointment was only deepened. The girl herself was to die the next year (June 9, 1859).

**The sick boy on the Piqué farm**

Now Dean Peyramale was off on another track. People were relating stories of a miracle in connection with Bernadette's visits to the Piqué farm. A little sick boy there had asked for her. Nine years old, he could neither eat nor close his mouth. It remained wide open like an oven. During Bernadette's visits he closed his mouth and recovered his taste for life. The Dean and an assistant curate went to the farm on March 15. 'Noticeable improvement,' he noted on that day. But there had to be a much more 'radical' cure before he could give a definite answer on the matter or say, with St Augustine, '*Causa finita est*'.

Police pressure was exerted more emphatically on Bernadette. She stopped her visits to the farm, where the mouth of the little boy had opened wide once again.

**Another interrogation**

On March 18 Bernadette submitted to another, formal interrogation. She declared:

'I do not believe that I have cured anyone and, for that matter, I have done nothing to that end. I do not know if I will go back to the grotto any more' (H 5, p. 35).

'She does not seem to want to tangle with the local authorities,' concluded the police commissioner.

### The real problem

The real problem was no longer Bernadette herself so much as the crowd that continued to frequent the grotto. The candles multiplied. There were ten on March 18, nineteen on March 21. On March 23 a plaster Virgin, furnished by one Félix Maransin, was placed in the niche of the apparition. At last an illicit place of worship could be pointed out. There was a basis for legal action! Moreover, the people were drinking the water from the spring, which the pharmacist Pailhasson had declared to be 'dangerous'.

And yet the press had voiced a clear verdict. On the day after the 'big day', the editorial in *Lavedan* was clearcut and straightforward:

What disappointment! ... How these poor credulous people have been humiliated. ... How many of them have realized, all too late unfortunately, the ridiculousness of the behaviour and regretted their excessive credulity!

'The miracle is the amazing credulousness of this throng, who have not been undeceived even by the spectacle of their own disappointment,' trumpeted *Le Bagnérais*. Meanwhile *L'Ere impériale*, the official voice of the prefect, expressed regrets that the whole affair had not been cut short by sending 'the alleged saint of eleven' (sic) 'to the hospice as a sick person.'

The strange affair overturned all customary habits and all the best laid plans.

*Dean Peyramale*          *Police Commissioner Jacomet*

*The grotto in 1858 washed by the waters of the Gave*

# 4

# THE LAST APPARITIONS
# (MARCH 25—JULY 16, 1858)

In the small hours of March 25, the feast of the Annuncia-
tion, Bernadette was roused from her sleep by a new
'urge' to go to the grotto. Her parents wanted to stop her
but the urge was irresistible. Realizing this her parents
made her wait. But at 5:00 a.m. she was on her way.

## The apparition of March 25

This time she had firmly decided to get some answer to
give to Dean Peyramale. After the rosary, *Aquerò*
approached through the inner cavity. Bernadette, over-
come with joy, took great pains to pose the question, as
formal and polite as a bow.

'Mademoiselle, would you be so kind as to tell me who
you are, if you please?'

*Aquerò* smiled. She did not reply. Bernadette repeated
the question insistently a second and third time. *Aquerò*
was still smiling all the while. This time, however, Bernadette would not let her alone, because an answer was
the precondition laid down by the Dean for the building of
a chapel.

The fourth time Bernadette asked the question, *Aquerò*
stopped 'laughing'. Her joined hands opened out and

extended towards the ground. Then she joined them again around her bosom, raised her eyes to the sky, and said:
*Que soy era Immaculada Councepciou*.


## The Immaculate Conception

Colour came back to Bernadette's face. She hastened towards the rectory, continually repeating the words lest she forget them, as she had the words about the procession. She avoided all questions and kept repeating to herself: *Immaculada Coun ... cet-tiou, Immaculada Coun ... cet-ciou*. She kept stumbling over the final two syllables. Finally she arrived at the rectory and fairly blurted out to Dean Peyramale:
*Que soy era Immaculada Councepciou*.

Peyramale staggered from shock. He was on the verge of saying: 'Vain little creature, you are the Immaculate Conception!' But the words stuck in his hoarse throat. He realized full well that Bernadette was not making this up herself. He was fighting against a blinding light, and his reason came to aid his resistance. The Virgin was conceived without sin, but she is not her conception. Finally, his words came out:

'A woman cannot have that name! You are mistaken! Do you know what that means?'

Bernadette shook her head: no.

'Then how can you say the words if you did not understand them?'

'I kept repeating them along the way.'

Peyramale felt all his anger slipping away. What strange movement was shaking his chest? Was he ill? No, he was holding in his sobs.

'She still wants the chapel,' murmured Bernadette in the silent room.

The Dean mobilized his last reserves of authority to save face.

'Go back home. I will see you another day.'

Bernadette was baffled. Why was the Dean angry? And what did the words mean? She didn't understand them at all. She had never heard them before, as such. But she found them very beautiful and gay. To be sure, the expression *Immaculée Conception* had floated into her ears in Church, on the feast day of December 8. But the words were uttered in a foreign language, French, which Bernadette did not know. And the concept itself was as unknown to her as was the mystery of the Trinity. She would learn the meaning of the term *Immaculada Councepciou* only that evening, at the home of Estrade. He was the first to even think of explaining it to her.

So, it was the Blessed Virgin then! At last Bernadette could abandon herself to the joy that had invaded her that morning.

But the form of the words was upsetting. Peyramale had a fine time formulating his theological objections in the letter he wrote to the bishop that evening. The 'believers' were annoyed by the unaccustomed expression. Each corrected Bernadette in his or her own way, adapting the expression to suit themselves. They made out that she said:

'I am the Virgin Immaculate.'

'I am Mary Immaculate.'

'I am the Virgin of the Immaculate Conception.'

Or, strictly speaking:

'Mary, the Immaculate Conception.'

They all reduced the disconcerting phrase to more familiar models.

Once his letter was written and his duty to his bishop was done, Peyramale himself felt the weight of the whole thing slipping off his shoulders. The child could not have made this up. It could have had, it must have had some meaning. He thought of the figures of speech he had learned in the seminary. Thus one could say, 'It is whiteness itself,' instead of saying, 'It is very white.' What was the name of that figure of speech? And how might it be applied to the dogma promulgated in Rome four years earlier:

We define that the Blessed Virgin was preserved from every taint of original sin ... from the first moment of her conception.

Light suddenly began to creep over the inner certitude which had been in his heart all the time, prior to any real calculation.

### The seventeenth apparition (April 7, 1858)

On Easter Tuesday, April 6, Bernadette again felt drawn to the grotto. She entered the confessional after Vespers. Antoinette Tardhivail, the assistant sacristan, saw her go in and suspected something. She confided her guess to some girlfriends under the seal of secrecy. The word spread like a train of gunpowder.

Bernadette's friends were worried. The prosecutor had interrogated her for four hours the previous week and had forbidden her to return to the grotto (D5, p. 75). Before Vespers, however, Bernadette had journeyed to the home of Blazy, the former mayor of Adé (4 kilometres from Lourdes). He had been healed at the grotto and wanted to see her. Blazy's son offered to take her during his break. It was a providential alibi.

The next morning, Easter Wednesday, Bernadette was at the grotto before dawn. A few hundred people were already there, and soon there would be 1000.

Bernadette was already in ecstasy amid an impressive air of silence. But there was a hubbub at the fringe of the crowd, heavy footsteps, and an authoritative voice. Someone was approaching the coveted spot.

'Let me through.'

It was Doctor Dozous, who had wanted to examine the ecstasy for some time. A fire lieutenant as well as medical doctor, he had had one of his 'men', Martin Tarbès, alert him. Dozous made his way through the crowd amid protests. Contrary to the respectful custom already inaugurated at the grotto, he kept his hat on. He moved forward and faced the crowd with conviction.

'I don't come as an enemy but in the name of science. I hurried here at a run (for a moment he uncovered his head, trickling with perspiration that glistened in the glow of the candles) and I cannot expose myself to draughts of air. I am the only one who can verify the religious event that is taking place here. Let me pursue this study.'

He sponged his head, annoyed that he might have done the wrong thing by running. Suddenly a strange phenomenon attracted his attention and caused him to forget everything else. This particular day Bernadette had a long candle standing on the ground. It had been given to her by Blazy, her host of the previous day. To protect the flame from the wind, her two hands were on either side of the stem. She was holding the candle between her wrists. Her fingers were enveloping the lighted wick closely, like the two valves of a shellfish. Through the partly closed fingers the flame could be seen licking her curved palms.

'She's burning!' cried someone in the crowd.

'Leave her alone,' cried Dozous.

He did not believe his eyes. After the ecstasy was over, he examined the two hands of the visionary. She had no idea what was going on.

'*Nou ya pas arré!*' exclaimed Dozous. 'There's nothing wrong!' Faith had won in an instant. With the impetuous exuberance that was characteristic of him, Dozous proclaimed the prodigious event to all in the *Café français*, to everyone in town, and to the police commissioner himself. The latter furtively noted down the doctor's excited remarks:

For me it was supernatural to see Bernadette on her knees before the grotto, in ecstasy, holding a lighted candle and covering the flame with her two hands, without her seeming to have the least impression of her hands' contact with the flame. I examined her hands. Not the slightest trace of burns.

### Visionaries galore (April 13—July 11, 1858)

After that date Bernadette withdrew into the shadows.
She was threatened. The prefect wanted to have done with
this grotto. His plan was to have the girl hospitalized as a
mentally ill patient. On May 4 he came to Lourdes to
preside over a review board. He declared forthrightly:

'Any person who claims to see visions will be immediately arrested and brought to the hospital in Tarbes.'

The very same day the police commissioner stripped the
grotto (an unauthorized place of worship!) of the religious
objects with which it had been decorated. Bernadette's
protective friends whisked her away. On March 8, without
a word, she was sent to the waters of Cauterets for her
asthma. There she quickly became the focal point of interest. Throughout the day people asked for prayers from
her. But the police commissioner of that town, who was in
charge of the surveillance over her, could only confirm her
discretion and her refusal 'of any and every sort of recompense' (D 2, p. 33).

In Lourdes itself the temperature climbed. Bernadette's
absence proved that she was not the cause of this. The
problem was the confounded grotto! 'Believers' regarded
the dismantling of May 4 as a sacrilege, and the spring
attracted them. Pailhasson, the pharmacist, had oppor-
tunely declared the latter 'dangerous.' Now along came
Latour, the pharmacist from Trie, and found in it 'special
curative properties which will make it rank among those
waters that constitute the mineral wealth of our province'
(D 2, p. 34). This rave notice helped to nurture a dream of
Mayor Lacadé: The erection of a thermal spa. His reports
allowed the enticing scheme to leak out. Unfortunately,
serious laboratory analysis was to show that the water of
the grotto spring was quite ordinary, devoid of all the
properties so earnestly envisioned by the municipality.

But the people who made their pilgrimages resisted all
efforts at dissuasion. These were organized spontaneously.
There were prayers, hymns, candles, devotions, proces-
sions. The guilds of Lourdes had taken over the manage-

ment of the grotto. Right after the water appeared, Tarbès, the wheelwright, and Domengieux, the carpenter, dug a channel for it. On April 10 they fashioned a basin with clumps of turf. On April 24 Castérot, a tinsmith, installed a zinc basin with three spigots. The carpenter then fashioned a board with holes in it to hold the ever increasing number of candles. And the quarrymen traced out trails in the steep slope that descends to the grotto.

Sergeant D'Angla couldn't get over it. These people, usually out for what they could get, gave their time and money for free. Gifts flowed in to the grotto: gold and silver hearts, statues, a gauze veil, and even a hunk of cheese. People gave everything they'd got. Money was deposited daily in the cracks and crevices of the grotto. By whom? What for? No one knew. Jacomet found a gold piece there. What substantial citizen left that gift? No substantial citizen at all: a poor old woman in desperate need had given her savings for a rainy day. 'It's for the Virgin,' she said.

'The richest offerings come from the poorer people,' noted the commissioner.

And the money was respected. It remained there without anyone trying to profit from it. At one point Jacomet thought he had uncovered an embezzlement scheme. On March 1 the money had disappeared from the grotto. However, investigation turned up nothing but a pious initiative. Fourcade, the sacristan, had collected the money and counted it. Then he had brought it to Dean Peyramale to say a Mass on 'the big day'. The collecting had gone on ever since then in a regular and yet spontaneous fashion.

Now, however, there were other phenomena of a more debatable and disturbing cast. The praying had started out with the accustomed forms, the rosary in particular. But people's fervour, frustrated by the end of the apparitions, now sometimes took on a feverish pitch.

On April 11, four days after the last public apparition to Bernadette, five women went to get a ladder on the Espélugues' farm. Fascinated by the mysterious caverns of

Massabielle, they raised the ladder on the right side of the grotto at the back, the side opposite the spring. Seeing a narrow crevice in the vault, the women climbed through it with great difficulty and disappeared. All five of them were carrying candles. A few minutes later they all climbed back down, proclaiming that they had seen the Virgin. They were church members of good reputation, and Peyramale actually gave them a better reception than he had given Bernadette.

On April 16, an expedition mounted by the police commissioner would find the clue to this mystery. After proceeding about ten metres in this rocky recess (*which Bernadette never did*), today's cave specialist will find the same thing that was found by the alleged visionaries and the police: a white stalactite in the form of a statue—but without a head. The play of shadow and light and imagination supplied what was missing. The solution of this puzzle did not stop the epidemic of visionaries. In June they were to multiply among the ranks of the school children. By the beginning of July the count was up to fifty or more (for details see D 2, pp. 56–87).

### The grotto put out-of-bounds

The officials did not wait until then to step in. On June 13, the grotto was declared out-of-bounds and barricaded. This repression exasperated the population of Lourdes. The barricades erected on June 15 were demolished on June 17—by one of the people whom the police commissioner *had requisitioned* to erect them! Erected again on June 18, they were demolished on the night of June 27. They were erected yet again on June 28, demolished on the night of July 4, and erected again on July 10.

Verbal reprimands rained down on the visitors as the police took down names and addresses. But they squeezed through the disjointed boards. The pure prayer of the apparitions period degenerated into pretence and superstitious, feverish rites.

## The first episcopal intervention (July 11)

Now the church authorities stepped in. On July 8, Dean Peyramale alerted the bishop of Tarbes. On July 11, Bishop Laurence, who had tried to keep his hopes up, denounced the abuses. Much to everyone's astonishment, they disappeared in the twinkling of an eye. There were to be no more problems with visionaries at the grotto.

## The final meeting (July 16, 1858)

Bernadette, now forgotten, had stayed completely out of this feverish business. She respected the order promulgated and counselled people against crossing the barricades.

Five days after the episcopal intervention that had restored peace and quiet, it was the feast of Our Lady of Mount Carmel. Bernadette suddenly felt drawn to Massabielle. Caught once again between the claims of obedience and the invincible attraction of the grotto, Bernadette compromised a little. She waited until the evening. Then, camouflaged in a dark-coloured hood that she had borrowed, she hastened through the twilight. But instead of going towards the Pont Vieux, which led down to Massabielle, she took the opposite direction. She stayed on the right bank and entered the Ribère meadow. Groups of people were there on their knees, praying silently in the direction of the barricaded grotto across the way. Bernadette knelt down, too, and lit her candle. It was one flame among many in the gathering darkness. She had come alone with her Aunt Lucile. Two other parishioners joined them silently.

The rosary was scarcely begun when Bernadette's hands opened wide in a greeting of joyous surprise. Her face went pale and lit up, as it had during the fifteen days of apparitions. She recited the rosary for a length of time that no one thought to measure. Then she got up. It was over.

This final apparition had been a silent one, like the first few. On the way back home Bernadette had only this to say:

> I saw neither the boards nor the Gave. It seemed to me that I was in the grotto, no more distant than the other times. I saw only the Holy Virgin.

It was the last time she would see her on this earth.

# 5

# WITNESS ON ALL FRONTS
## (1858–1860)

During the apparitions, Bernadette in ecstasy had been a witness without realizing it. The transfiguration of her face and the transport of her prayer had shaken and converted many onlookers, though Bernadette did not notice this (H 3, pp. 80–135).

During those moments Bernadette did not have to defend herself against questioners. She had not even heard those who might by chance try to communicate with her. She was cut off from the outside world.

When an apparition was over, however, the questions poured in from all sides. All the inquisitive questions and hypotheses, be they sober-minded or outlandish, were directed to her. In the course of the day she became the prey of questioners, both believers and unbelievers, admirers and adversaries. From February 21 on she underwent regular interrogations and cross-examinations by police officials, magistrates, doctors commissioned by the prefect to declare her mentally ill, and priests. The latter she feared the most, even as she feared God himself. Because she alone could tell people anything about the apparition and its message, this frail child became the caryatid on which rested the future of the pilgrimage, the chapel that was to be built, and everything else.

How did Bernadette get through it all without losing her calmness, her equilibrium, or her mind? Herein lies one of the astonishing aspects of the whole Bernadette phenomenon. She answered people without calculation or formulations, without fear or complacence. She spoke in the briefest and most direct terms, unwittingly carrying out the Gospel maxim: 'When they bring you before synagogues, rulers and authorities, do not worry about how to defend yourselves or what to say. The Holy Spirit will teach you at that moment all that should be said' (Lk 12:11–12).

Therein lay Bernadette's whole secret. That is how the little David withstood the Goliaths of Church and State. And those who did not surrender to her at least acknowledged her intelligence and her sincerity.

Of course she had supporters who helped her to extricate herself from difficulty in all the manoeuvres designed to demean her or show her up. Monsieur Dufo, a lawyer who was an ardent believer in the apparitions, began to warn her of certain traps about halfway through the fifteen days of apparitions. Judge Pougat, the President of the Tribunal, did so from a very different motive. Lost in the judiciary, into which he was propelled by political supporters, he warned Bernadette against illegal or irregular summonses from the imperial prosecutor, his subordinate. Dutour was aware of these warnings, but he did not know how to go about denouncing his superior. The notes that he scratched out on the subject bear witness to his embarrassment. But he was not so embarrassed to reproach the visionary herself:

'Beware, Bernadette. There is a certain gentleman near the portal who is giving you advice. He will not stop you from going to prison!'

Half in French and half in *patois*, Bernadette quickly responded:

'*Que deouét parla debout àou mème Moussu,*': 'You should speak directly to that gentleman.'

Her candour accomplished more than the advice she received. What was true of her ecstasy was also true of her testimony: her secret lay in nothing else but her transparency.

**First Communion**

Bernadette was now going to school. It offered her protection against intrusive people. On June 3 she made the First Communion which she had so greatly desired.

During the retreat Dean Peyramale had authorized a strange woman to approach Bernadette and ask her a question:

'Reverend Father forbids you to go to the grotto. What if the Virgin were to order you to go there, what would you do?'

'I would go back and ask Reverend Father for permission' (Letter of Peyramale: D 2, no. 314, p. 359).

The day after her Communion, Emmanuélite Estrade asked her another question:

'What made you happier: First Communion or the apparitions?' Her reply was simple and direct:

'The two things go together, but they cannot be compared. I was very happy with both' (A. Barbet, PONev 925).

**Cure-seekers and curiosity-seekers**

The summer brings to Lourdes, the crossroads of the roads and valley in the spa region, the usual file of holiday-making tourists, starting with the Emperor. The Parisian press has written about the apparitions. The rumour was sustained in pious bulletins, particularly in *Le Rosier de Marie*. The cure-seekers and the curious flock to Bernadette. She was the only recourse for those who wanted to find out the facts and to form a judgment.

In the Gaol, life was disorganized by perpetual visits. Every day the Soubirous resisted people's efforts, one more ingenious than the next, to leave some offering. Bernadette was adamant, and not without flashes of temper. One day some wealthy visitors asked her little brother to go for some water in the grotto. On his return he was given a gold piece for his trip. When he got back to the Gaol, very proud of the money he had earned, he got a royal box on the ear from his sister. He had to go and give back the money at once. He himself recounted this incident.

In July Charles Madon, a young lawyer from Beaune, noted down his conversation with Bernadette on the spot. He was won over immediately by her physiognomy. She was 'intelligent, gracious, and modest—a pleasure to look at'. But her asthma disturbed him. She 'coughed' frequently. He asked her some questions.

'Have you prayed for your own cure?'

'No.'

'And your secrets? What are they about?'

'They concern only me.'

'If the Pope were to ask you for them, would you tell them to him?'

'No.'

'What if your confessor would not let you receive Communion during Eastertide because of your refusal?'

'No.'

'I know one of your secrets. It is that you will be a nun.'

Bernadette laughed:

'It's not that. They are more serious.'

'Does it bother you that people ask for your secrets?'

'No, but the apparition told me not to tell them.'

Through able questioning, however, the visitor did manage to find out some things about the secrets. They were spoken 'in *patois* ... on several different days'. They concerned only 'her own life'. On other occasions she was to say that they did not concern the pilgrimage, or France, or the world. That was what justified her discretion.

On July 17, Bishop Thibault of Montpellier landed in Lourdes. He asked to see Bernadette and Dean Peyramale eagerly summoned her to the rectory. Her poverty and simplicity made a deep impression on the bishop. He would have liked her to take a little offering from him. No, thank you. Then what about this beautiful rosary that was indulgenced by Pope Pius IX himself? No, thank you. If she didn't want a gift, then how about trading her rosary for this one?

'No, Reverend Father, I prefer my own rosary.'

Throughout the conversation Bernadette addressed the visitor as 'Reverend Father.' She did not know that he was a bishop any more than she knew what the mystery of the Trinity was two months earlier. The whole atmosphere and pageant of this meeting was far less impressive to her than was her visit to the Tarbes seminary. Then, she had run to the window of the parlour and looked out in astonishment at all the men in cassocks: 'Oh! Oh!'

On July 20, Bishop Cardon de Garsignies of Soissons asked for her. He questioned her about heaven. Had she not experienced it? Her reply was simply: 'I know nothing, Monseigneur. I am ignorant.'

Like his colleague from Montpellier, he left Lourdes disturbed, challenged, bolstered in his inner convictions and, finally, convinced.

The two bishops hastened to tell what they knew to Bishop Laurence of Tarbes. They urged him to get involved. And so, on July 28, at 11:00 a.m., he signed a formal document establishing a commission of inquiry.

On the same day the wife of Admiral Bruat, governess of the imperial prince, came to Lourdes with her children, a priest and a nun. They had a conversation with Bernadette.

Since the Virgin was married to Saint Joseph, she should have had a ring, shouldn't she? asked the priest.

'No, Father, she didn't have one.'

The Sister asked Bernadette to take them to the grotto, but she refused.

'No! No! I am forbidden.'

It was not hard for the party to find a guide because the believers were on holiday. Just for spite, some of them had given the alert to Callet, the rural constable, who was supposed to accost violators of the ordinance and take down their names and addresses for the police record. The believers would have liked to have seen Callet get into a real jam by accosting such important visitors. Awakened from his after-lunch nap, Callet arrived at the grotto and saw the women praying despite the 'no entrance' signs. He suddenly sensed the trap, as a private might who is just about to hit a general in civvies. Amiably he noted down the identity of the visitor in his own inimitable spelling: 'Amral Bruhat's widow, govorniss of the children of France and her family in the company of a sistir.'

To save face and reputation, he climbed over the rock and dropped down inside the barricaded grotto in order to throw the bouquets left there into the Gave. It was one of his daily duties; a sad duty but at least it gave him an alibi. The Admiral's wife was a great lady, and she noticed his confusion.

'Guard, Sir, would you be so kind as to fill this carafe with water from the spring for me?'

He did so quite readily, and also gave her the clods of earth and a few stones she asked for. He refused the 100-sou coin that the Sister wanted to give him. That evening the Admiral's widow arranged to have the money placed in his home while he was out, so that he could not refuse it.

While she was still in prayer at the grotto, Louis Veuillot, editor of *L'Univers*, arrived in a white hat. Callet took down his name too, as Veuillot exclaimed: 'And so they want to stop people from praying to the good God here!' (D 3, p. 46)

He went back to Lourdes and arranged a meeting with Bernadette at the house of Pailhasson, the pharmacist and chocolate seller. He conducted a regular interview before a large audience. Father Pomian translated for him. He kept insisting on the secrets, though Bernadette resisted and Father Pomian kept trying to dissuade him: 'That's not important.' Veuillot was very moved. After Bernadette left, he wrote: 'She is illiterate, but she is worth more than I' (D 3, p. 47).

A month later in Paris, on August 28, the interview was to fill five columns on page one of *L'Univers*.

On July 30, Father Hyacinthe Loison subjected Bernadette to a regular cross-examination. At that time a famous preacher, he was to renounce his vows later on.

During the same period Father Nègre, a pious Jesuit, employed all the tools of his theology to prove to Bernadette that she 'saw the devil.'

'*Et diáble n'ey pas aoutá beróy qu'éro,*' replied Bernadette: 'The devil is not as beautiful as she.'

According to the demonology of the visitor, Satan was facile in undergoing metamorphoses but was unable to disguise all his attributes. He had bestial characteristics and hid them.

'You did not see the feet. Her feet were hidden.'

'Yes, I did. She had bare feet, very pretty.'

'You didn't see the hands! They were hidden in the shadows, weren't they?'

'No, I saw them and they were very nice' (A VII, p. 264).

At this point Bernadette broke off the interview with this remark to Antoinette Tardhivail: '*N'at bo créde, tournéns-en*': 'He doesn't wish to believe. Let's get out of here.'

The dialogue in this conversation, reported by Antoinette, might seem highly improbable. Twenty years later, however, Father Nègre unwittingly acknowledged that that had indeed been his idea and his line of thought. Replying to Father Cros in a letter dated September 18, 1878, he writes:

> I know (sic) that in his appearances the Devil ordinarily takes the feet of some beast.

> Since the Incarnation ... God does not deign to permit the Devil to take the full and perfect form of humanity. He must betray himself by some bestial characteristic (A VI).

Other interrogators threatened Bernadette with hell fire (D 5, p. 292), dragged her to perilous theological heights, or tried to trap her in the inextricable toils of casuistry. She replied clearly and briefly—right to the point, as did

Joan of Arc. The following dialogue took place between Bernadette and a missionary in the Tarbes diocese:

'Since the Holy Virgin promised you heaven, you need not worry about taking care of your soul.'

'Oh, Reverend Father! I will go to heaven if I do as one ought.'

'But what do you mean by "doing as one ought"?'

'Oh! I don't have to tell someone like you that, Reverend Father!'

Others were to ask her to do impossible things, such as duplicating the smile of the Virgin.

Bernadette was under a severe handicap in giving her testimony. Until the beginning of that year she had only spoken the dialect of her valley. French was a foreign language to her, and so there were misunderstandings and errors. Realizing this, Bernadette made an effort to speak French from July on. She spoke 'a very incorrect French,' noted Balech de Lagarde, when he came to interview the new celebrity for *Courrier français* on September 24. The journalist earned his pay, questioning Bernadette about everything: 'The country is talking about you a great deal ... Does that please you?'

'It doesn't matter to me.'

'Several journals have printed your name. Have you been told this?'

'Yes.'

'Have you seen the journals?'

'No, I can scarcely read at all.'

'Do you like that?'

'Oh, not at all, no!'

Then the journalist tried to 'dazzle' her, to use his own expression: 'Listen, Bernadette, you must come to Paris with me. In three weeks you will be rich ... I will take care of your good fortune.'

'Oh, no, no! I want to remain poor.'

His urgings were in vain.

On October 5, 1858 the Emperor was on holiday. He was under pressure from the Lourdes affair, and ordered the barricades to be removed from the grotto. The measure earned him great popularity.

## Facing the episcopal commission

The commission of inquiry appointed by the bishop set to
work. On November 17, Bernadette was subjected to her
first ecclesiastical interrogation. She displayed the same
limpid assurance before the four canons. She unhesitat-
ingly distinguished between what she knew and what she
had forgotten: dates, for example. The message itself,
however, was very much present to her. On only one point
was her memory a blank: the famous procession requested
by the apparition on March 2. Her recollection of it had
disintegrated under the ire of Dean Peyramale. She could
only say: 'I am not sure that this order was given to me;
but in regard to the construction of the chapel, I have
always been sure and I am still certain now' (B 1, p. 194).

In mid-September the Soubirous family left the Gaol
for a more wholesome room in Deluc's place. He ran a
pastry and coffee shop, and he was vaguely related to the
Soubirous through the Castérot family. So the family had
now heeded the warning given by the three doctors who
came and hurriedly examined Bernadette on Thursday,
March 4: 'If you want to preserve your children, you must
not remain here' (H 5, p. 354, note 280).

## The Gras mill (1859)

During the first quarter of 1859, the Gras mill was vacant
and François Soubirous again tried his luck there. It was
there that a young English tourist, R. S. Standen, met
Bernadette on April 19. François had regained his craft
and his dignity. He seemed quite 'respectable', noted the
visitor. And Bernadette was a 'pretty looking girl'. She
spoke 'very intelligently' as she explained the functioning

of the mill, familiar to her from early childhood. It was good for her to find herself out in the open air again, beside a brook. Her asthma was much better.

The young man was particularly struck by the fact of Bernadette's complete unconcern about the miracles which the whole town was talking about. The English youth mentioned a few to her. Bernadette, totally put off, rejected them all with one outburst: 'There's no truth in all that' (D 5, p. 51, note 124).

Between August 8 and August 12, an overworked Bernadette was suffering from another bout of asthma. Dominique Mariote and Paul de Lajudie found her confined to bed. They took advantage of the opportunity to question her at length. Each of the two men made his own separate notes of the interview (B 1, pp. 202–210).

'Why were you forbidden to go to the grotto?'

'Because everyone was following me.'

'Why is it that you no longer go there now?'

'Oh, back then, I was really pushed to go!' (Said with great emphasis, notes Mariote here.)

'You were really pushed?'

'Yes, I was really pushed!'

'But who was pushing you?'

'I don't know, but I was being pushed and I could not stay away.'

'And now you are no longer pushed?'

'No, Father.'

'Have you seen the Holy Virgin since then?'

'No, Father, I haven't seen her.'

'Not even on the day of your First Communion?'

'No, Father.'

'When did you make your First Communion?'

'Last year.'

'And when you go to the grotto, you do not see her any more?'

'No, Father.'

They questioned her at length about her secrets, but to no avail. When she bade them goodbye, it was with a natural and amiable smile (D 5, pp. 318–319; B 1, p. 211).

One of the two, Paul de Lajudie, returned to question her on September 28:

'Would you tell your secret to the Pope?'

'The Holy Virgin forbade me to tell it to any perso.1 ... The Pope is a person.'

'But the Pope has the power of Jesus Christ!'

'Yes, the Pope is very powerful on earth, but the Holy Virgin is powerful in heaven.'

He, too, noted Bernadette's complete indifference to the miracles.

'To your knowledge, have there been miraculous events, cures worked miraculously?'

'I have been told that there have been miracles; but to my knowledge, no!'

He expressed his astonishment. Bernadette became more explicit.

'Not to my personal knowledge. I have not seen them.'

'People say that you have contributed to some of these miracles. Is that true?'

Smiling, she replied: 'Oh no, Sir, not a one!'

To help her asthma and to give her refuge from these importunities, Bernadette was sent to the waters of Cauterets again that year.


## A fourfold life

During this period Bernadette was living four lives:

1.  She was working to earn bread for her family, spending whole days as a 'little nurse-maid' at the home of Armantine Grenier (D 6, p. 74, note 180).
2.  She was helping out at home and playing her role as the eldest child, particularly vis-a-vis the madcap Toinette.
3.  Prevented from attending school regularly, she was trying to make up for being behind with the help of kind lessons from Antoinette Tardhivail.

4. Finally, she was answering questions for all sorts of visitors, whether she met them at her home or was summoned elsewhere to see them: e.g., to the rectory, the hospice, the *Hôtel des Pyrénées*, and private homes. Her testimony was a deciding factor in the establishment of the place of pilgrimage during the work of the episcopal commission.

'Available to everyone, she edified some and astounded or disconcerted others,' noted Dean Peyramale in his letter of May 17, 1860 (D 6, p. 110). As Father Pomian put it, she herself was 'the best proof of the apparition' (PANev 1142). But at what a price!

It was not only her gift for repartee but also the natural economy of her responses that saved her. She responded directly to the question asked her, never going further. She was completely indifferent to the effect she produced. She made no effort to convince people, avoiding debate and discouraging lengthy discussion. She knew how to unwind naturally, and this spared her much useless fatigue.

The aptness of her remarks and her behaviour astonished all those who knew her. Some of them had noted that she never displayed so much intelligence as she did in giving her testimony. This charisma, evident most fully when Bernadette faced the authorities (see Lk 12:11), was also present when she met visitors of all sorts during the course of an ordinary day. It enabled her to avoid enormous risks.

But it was an impossible life for the Soubirous. At the mill their natural generosity was dangerously gaining the upper hand again. They were too receptive, too accommodating, both to their customers and to the visitors from whom they would accept nothing. Louise again began to offer people a collation, and to say to customers in a tight fix: 'You'll pay when you can.'

*The hospice-school in Lourdes where Bernadette lived*

# 6

# BERNADETTE UNDER PROTECTION

**Dominiquette concerned**

At the beginning of 1860, Dominiquette Cazenave was concerned about the confusion in Bernadette's life. She sought out Dean Peyramale: 'You are not going to leave her in the world!' (A VII, p. 73).

Dean Peyramale had been thinking about the matter. As early as the summer of 1858, he had suggested to Bernadette that he might be able to let her live with the Sisters who ran the hospice. But she had replied: 'Oh, I understand exactly what you mean, Reverend Father; but I love my mother and father so much!' (D 3, p. 326).

Now the project began to take definite shape. Mayor Lacadé, who subsidized the hospice, thought of a special status for Bernadette. She could be taken in as an indigent sick person (D VI, p. 77). But under the cover of this administrative formula, arrangements would be made so that she could pursue her studies at the hospice school.

Her parents were averse to the idea of separation from Bernadette, even as she was averse to parting from them. They were promised that their daughter would come to see them freely, but in the company of a nun (BARBET, pp. 129–30; D 6, p. 77).

**With the Sisters**

On Sunday, July 15, Bernadette was installed in the hospice, where she was to stay until she left Lourdes. She was protected at last, a step that was necessary in one sense but also unfortunate in another sense. For her testimony now lost something of its vivacity and freedom. She could no longer deftly deal with people as she once did in her own natural way. Now she was living under the watchful eye of the nuns and the more distant surveillance of Dean Peyramale. She was the visionary who was led into the parlour and presented to visitors in humiliating terms. For the pedagogy of that day insisted on repressing pride in every circumstance that might prompt one to indulge in it. Thus Bernadette was submitted to alternating doses of admiration and humiliation that would have shattered a less solid character.

Her keen lack of self-interest also lost its edge. In Bernadette's absence the family became less scrupulous on this point. Thus in October 1860, after Bernadette had left home, Azun de Bernétas finally managed to get Louise to accept money to defray expenses for her trips to the grotto on his behalf. He had asked her to make a novena there for him. It was, of course, fair compensation for the time she spent doing this, when she might have been earning money for food; and it had taken a great deal of persuasion on his part. But the fact remains that such remuneration would have been out of the question if Bernadette had still been living at home.

She herself no longer had the right to refuse 'dishonest money'. She had to accept it for work, and that cost her more than anything else. But in that area as in everything else, she was trained to be obedient and to fight against her own instincts. She was never really permitted to make her own decisions.

Finally, Bernadette left her own milieu. There were no longer any boarders in the poor children's class that she had been attending, and she must now choose between the 'first class' composed of middle-class girls and the 'second class' attended by less affluent but decent girls. On her own request she was put into the latter class.

The advantage for her was that now, for the first time in

her life, she was going to attend a regular year of school. It was not easy for her, because she was now sixteen years old and not used to that kind of effort. She sometimes despaired when she found that the things she had so painstakingly memorized quickly vanished from her mind:

'You would have to cram the book into my head!'

She was more at ease with needlework. The intelligence and expertise of her hands proved to be exceptional, especially in embroidery.

'At recreation she was the life of the party. Always gay, she breathes life into the play of the younger classes, though she quickly gets out of breath' (testimony of Sister Philomène Camès, B 1, p. 239).

## Bernadette's 'faults'

Seeing her day after day, the nuns learned to recognize her 'faults.' She knew what she wanted. Her bouts of stubbornness astonished them. One day she held out against Sister Victoire Poux, who wanted her to change her Sunday dress (for no good reason). When they refused to let her go home to her family, she protested: 'You promised me.'

But at least she protested only in private, never 'in the presence of the children' (A VII, p. 191, no. 136). Sensitive to little injustices, she was quick to defend others against the mistakes made by those in charge. That was viewed as a weakness, and her prankishness was not at all appreciated as proper to a 'seer.'

The latter trait posed the greatest obstacle to her canonization later on. The most serious incident occurred in the early summer of 1861. Bernadette was on the first floor of the hospice with Julie Garros (aged ten), a very lively little girl. She was Bernadette's tutor for lessons, though she was the younger one. The window looked out on the kitchen garden, where the two girls noticed some enticing strawberries. They were formally forbidden to go into that garden, but no one had ever said specifically that they could not collect strawberries. Bernadette had an idea:

'I will throw my shoe out the window. You go get it and bring back some strawberries' (D 6, p. 81).

During the beatification process for Bernadette, the devil's advocate stressed the gravity of this incident. Speaking in Latin, he noted that this was 'undoubtedly *malitia* and a patent violation of discipline'. *Malitia* means a deliberate inclination to do evil. Fortunately for Bernadette it was a sin of youth that she would redeem with her later life.

Sister Victorine was astonished to see that Bernadette entertained fancies about her dress and was concerned with beauty care. One day she found her trying to 'widen her skirt' after the pattern of the crinolines that Dean Peyramale and the clergy were calling 'diabolic'. Another time Bernadette was caught trying to add a piece of wood to her corset as a stay (D 6, p. 82, note 212).

Bernadette was seventeen at the time, and the stirrings of nature were not foreign to her. In those days such behaviour posed a problem. Today the absence of such behaviour would be more disturbing.

On the other hand all recognized her respect for God, the seriousness of her prayer, and her exacting demands on herself and her sisters. But on one occasion Sister Victorine got a very bad impression when she heard Bernadette telling her sister Antoinette the following: 'Don't learn to read.'

Bernadette was speaking to her near a window in the corridor of the hospice. Sister Victorine, who just happened to catch the conversation in passing, was astonished by this bad advice and spoke to Bernadette.

'Ah, we are from a family where that is worth more,' was Bernadette's reply.

Sister Victorine did not pursue the matter further. What Bernadette feared in the case of her sister was the bad example of other young ladies. They would hide cheap novels in their missal and read them on the sly (B 1, 242). But Bernadette wouldn't tattle on them for all the money in the world.

The hardest thing to repress in her was her repugnance towards money. At first she would 'let it fall on the ground'. Now she would say, in a scarcely encouraging tone: 'There is a poor-box.'

And if, despite all her efforts, the money ended up in her hands, she hurriedly made sure that it would be passed into the hands of the Mother Superior.

She was attached to nothing and readily gave away what she had (D 6, p. 84). Gifts and personal objects did not accumulate in her little wardrobe. Nothing special or peculiar could be found in it, except the flask of wine that astounded Sister Victorine. Her parents brought her some wine now and then 'to fortify her,' according to the accepted local formula.

If Bernadette took snuff, it was because Doctor Balencie had prescribed it for her asthma. But it caused several incidents. One day during class she offered a pinch to her neighbours. Their cascade of sneezes provoked the year's wildest fit of laughing.

Bernadette brought gaiety wherever she went. Indeed she brought just a bit too much, according to the opinion current in her day. At recreation she fled from all serious subjects, even right after meetings of the Children of Mary. She preferred play and good fun. She took more delight in giving pleasure to others than to herself, except when her companions asked her to give an account of the apparitions.

'Oh, please leave me be,' she implored, 'I must tell it to so many strangers' (PATarb 283, D 7, p. 29).

## Some acknowledged good qualities

She was closely watched to protect her from the curious. Her piety was ordinary but irreproachable. She always made her Sign of the Cross as she did 'during the apparitions', even when she was alone. This action was very edifying. She was officially permitted to go to Communion every Sunday and even now and then during the week. In that particular era such frequent Communion was a privilege (D 6, p. 83, notes 216–217).

People also respected her scrupulousness about not taking a throat lozenge the evening before she was to receive Communion, even if she had a cough. She did not want to risk breaking her fast. On that point she was only observing the ordinary teaching of the time.

But Bernadette had no talent for prayer, as she readily admitted: 'Oh dear! I don't know how to meditate.'

'She buckled down to it in the long run,' added Sister Victorine (A VII, p. 191, no. 136; RSL, no. 15, p. 106).

**The worst trial**

Around the end of 1861, Bernadette was photographed for the first time. Father Bernardou, professor of chemistry in the minor seminary, obtained Dean Peyramale's permission to take her picture.

Like a demanding film director, he insisted that Bernadette adopt exactly the same pose and expression that she had during the apparitions. Bernadette protested vigourously: 'But she isn't here!'

Father Bernardou would hear no such talk. He was completely taken up with his project.

Did those involved permit him to preserve her image because they were afraid of losing it altogether? Periodic crises with her asthma raised fears about how long she had to live. She could not breathe, and the air accumulated in her lungs choked her. She would flush and turn purple. The first time this happened, her parents were summoned during the night (testimony of Jean-Marie Soubirous, PONev, 164v; D 7, p. 112, note 623).

Was that her worst trial? No, according to her own words during one such crisis: 'I prefer that to receiving visits' (D 7, p. 112).

Visitors came by the hundreds, then by the thousands. It

became intolerable, to the point of nausea. Bernadette was very reluctant to meet the visitors, especially when they interrupted her recreation. Sister Victorine tells us about it:

> I saw her begin to cry in the doorway, when there were 20 or 30 or 40 people in the drawing room waiting for her ... These big tears would come. I would say to her: Courage!

Bernadette would wipe away her tears, enter the room, greet everyone graciously, and then answer their questions (A VII, p. 197, no. 167; RSL, no. 15, p. 108). Then she would return to her play as if nothing had happened (PATarb, p. 229, no. 49).

The most painful thing for her was to be treated as a saint, though she herself did nothing to encourage such treatment. People would ask her to touch holy objects.

'I am forbidden to do that.'

Then people would resort to subterfuges. Even distinguished visitors would drop a rosary so that she might pick it up for them. Her clear-headedness and keenness would neutralize her sense of obligation. One day she said: 'I'm not the one who dropped it.'

Another time, Sister Victorine tells us, several women approached her from behind: 'If I could only cut off a bit of her dress!'

'What imbeciles you are!' said the visionary (A VII, p. 197).

Now that Bernadette knew how to write, the forced labour of writing documents in her own hand or signing them was added to her other duties. She began her new job on January 1, 1859, when she was ordered to write several copies of model prayers and aspirations none of which she understood. She soon found her own master formula: p.p. Bernadette. This abbreviated autograph, which she wrote on hundreds of pictures, means: 'Pray for Bernadette.'

People often presented their rosaries for her to bless. 'I

do not wear a stole,' she would tell them. And she was asked about her secrets day after day: 'If you cannot tell them, it is a useless revelation', argued three Jesuits.

'It is useful for me,' she replied.

'Why have you hidden them from your confessor?' asked Father Cabane.

'They are no sin,' replied Bernadette.

### The final episcopal interrogation

On December 7, 1860, Bernadette was summoned for a solemn and final interrogation before Bishop Laurence in the Tarbes chancery. The bishop's face was a smooth, imperturbable mass. He was surrounded by the sharply chiselled faces of the twelve members of the commission. The Secretary, Fourcade, tirelessly kept on filling up the big sheets of white paper in front of him.

'Did the Holy Virgin have a halo?' asked one of the commission members.

'A halo?'

Bernadette was not familiar with the word. When it was explained to her, she quickly replied: 'She was enveloped with a soft light.'

'Did you get a good look at it?'

'Oh, yes.'

'And did this light appear at the same time as the apparition?'

'It came before it and remained a little after it.'

'The idea of making you eat some kind of grass doesn't seem to me to be an idea worthy of the Holy Virgin,' remarked another member of the commission.

'Well, we eat salad all right,' replied Bernadette.

At the end of the interview she was asked to show exactly how the Virgin spoke the words of March 25: 'I am the Immaculate Conception.' Bernadette got up, stretched out her arms, and joined her hands. Something happened as they watch the enactment of this inspired gesture:

Two tears were seen running down the face of the old bishop. After the meeting, still deeply moved, he said to a vicar-general: 'Did you see that child?' (SEMPÉ, p. 201)

Thirteen months later, on January 18, 1862, the bishop issued his official letter recognizing the apparitions:

We judge that the Immaculate Mother of God truly appeared to Bernadette.

The judgment was solidly grounded on the spiritual fruits of the prilgrimage, the cures, and Bernadette herself.

## Bernadette and her doctor

Shortly afterwards, people again had reason to fear that they were going to lose her. On April 28, 1862, she received the sacrament of Extreme Unction. She did indeed seem to be *in extremis*, breathing her last. She could take communion the regular way. She managed to get a little morsel of the host down her throat with the help of a little water from the grotto.

Was it the end? No. The face of the dying girl changed. Her blocked breathing became more easy. Relieved, she smiled. She would have liked to eat, to get up out of bed. Mother Superior refused. There would be time enough for that tomorrow.

The next day, April 29, Doctor Balencie was rather surprised to find her in the parlour. He hid his astonishment: 'Well, well! The medicines we have prescribed have done their work!'

'But I didn't take them,' observed Bernadette (D 6, p. 360, no. 1300).

In the town, where reports of Bernadette's death agony had heightened emotions, there was now talk of a miracle.

But it was one of those sudden remissions common in cases of asthma. There was no mysticism whatsoever in Bernadette's own conclusion:

> If I am sick again, I will beg the doctor to pay close attention ... He took my illness for another, and I could have died (D 6, pp. 360–361).

The formal judgment of the bishop of Tarbes silenced those who were hostile to Bernadette. But now even more subtle questions were sometimes formulated: 'Suppose the bishop of Tarbes had judged that you were deluded, what would you have replied?' asked Father Corbin.

'I could never say that I did not see or hear what I did see and hear,' replied Bernadette.

The year 1862 brought her an occasion of great joy. At the end of August she met her godfather, Jean-Marie Védère, who was home on leave from the service. He had won the Legion of Honour medal in 1859 for his actions in the battle of Solferino. Bernadette met him for the first and last time, bathed in the glory of his legendary deeds and his remoteness.

The year 1863 went on in the monotonous rhythm of boarding-school life and enforced visits. In June of that year Bernadette met a visitor who really moved her. It was Father Alix. The famous and rather worldly orator had undergone the shock of a thorough conversion at Lourdes. He confided the story to Bernadette. She recognized her own experience in what he told her. Twice she exclaimed: 'It's the Blessed Virgin, Father, the Blessed Virgin, who did that' (D 7, p. 244, no. 1457).

In October 1863, her picture was taken for the second time, thanks to the tactful approach of an itinerant photographer, Billard-Perrin of Pau.

*Photos of Bernadette by Billard-Perrin (October 1863)*

*The statue of the apparition formally inaugurated on April 4, 1864*

# 7

# THE SHEPHERDESS AND THE SCULPTOR
## (1863–1864)

Now Bernadette was requisitioned for a matter of some delicacy. The Lacour ladies from Lyon were devoted adherents of Lourdes and they had had a chalet built for them on what is now the esplanade. They decided to replace the little statue which the people of Lourdes had placed in the grotto with a statue which was to be hewn out of Carrara marble. It would depict the apparition life-size, and it was to be 'as exact as possible'.

With the consent of the bishop of Lourdes they signed a contract with the sculptor, Joseph Fabisch, a member of the Lyon Academy of Sciences, Belles-Lettres, and Arts. It was a fabulous contract for 7,000 *francs-or*, plus his expenses. He was to begin with a trip to Lourdes to question Bernadette. Fabisch was a specialist on this particular subject, for it was he who had created the spire-statue for Notre Dame de Fourvière and the one of Notre Dame de la Salette.

**The first meeting**

On September 17, 1863 he arrived in Lourdes. Bernadette was summoned from recreation to meet him. The sculptor noted her features with an expert's eye:

Her figure, while not possessing the regularity sought
by the sculptor, has something very *simpatico* about it:
a charm that commands respect and inspires faith
(Memorandum of October 27, 1878, p. 3).

He was sympathetic, but he was also a bit on edge and
out of sorts. When making the La Salette statue he had
negotiated for permission to 'interpret' the 'eccentric'
pieces of information given by those who had seen the
Virgin. In this case, however, the contract obliged him to
conform to the information given by the visionary. But
might this not be contrary to the 'rules of art', which he
believed to be the last court of appeal? He prepared
twenty questions in pencil on a piece of notepaper, which
is extant today, and he recorded Bernadette's answers:
   'The body, erect or bent forward?'
   'Erect . . . without being stiff.'
   'Was the head inclined to one side or bent forward?'
   'Erect also.'
   'What about the hands? How did she join them when
she said: "I am the Immaculate Conception"?'
   Later the sculptor wrote the following:

Bernadette got up with the greatest simplicity. She
joined her hands and raised her eyes to heaven. I have
never seen anything more beautiful . . . Neither Mino
da Fiesole, nor Perugino, nor Raphael have ever done
anything so sweet and yet so profound as was the look
of that young girl, consumptive to her finger-
tips. . . . One could not have the least doubt in the
world about the signal favour that she had received
(Letter of September 17, 1863; D 7, p. 280, no. 1500).

Inspiration came to him at that moment. Anxious for
the contract, the sculptor went to the grotto with Bernadette. In the niche he drew a silhouette on paper to
determine the size and position of the statue. He also
showed Bernadette 'a portfolio of illustrations in which
the Holy Virgin is depicted in all sorts of ways . . . Ber-

nadette scarcely paid any attention to them. Then, all of a sudden, as we passed an engraving or lithograph of the Virgin of Saint Luke, she quickly put out her hand and said: "There is something there".'

This point, which has come down to us through two traditions, has fascinated Picasso and Malraux. But they disregarded, or were unaware of the contemporary testimony, which tells us what Bernadette quickly added:

'But that's not it! No, that's not it!' (See H 3, p. 214, no. 83; and my article in response to Malraux in *Figaro Littéraire*, April 13, 1974).

**The objections**

In November 1863, the sculptor sent Dean Peyramale a photo of his plaster model, which was about two-thirds of the projected size of the finished work. Peyramale's letter of reply suggests that Bernadette's criticisms had been severe:

> The figure does not seem young enough and does not smile enough. . . . The veil came straight down and was smooth. . . . The hands were more closely joined, the fingers right up against each other; the left foot was a little more to one side, etc.

Aware of the great gap between Bernadette's vision and that of the artist, and anxious to respect the latter's freedom, Peyramale added the following words to give him a clear field:

> I do not know whether the rules of art will permit you to pay heed to all these observations. I am convinced that you, inspired by your talent and the Immaculate Virgin, will present us with a remarkable work of art (D 7, p. 309, no. 1543).

The case containing the statue arrived in Lourdes on March 30, 1864, five days before the solemn ceremony of its inauguration. Bernadette was recovering from another bout of illness. She was beginning to get back to her games and her routine. She was summoned away from her play with the little girls and presented to Father Ollivier, a preacher in Notre-Dame. In his presence Dean Peyramale rebuked her, acting on the accustomed principle that 'humiliation is good for people'. She was with the two priests, looking at the statue which had been set up on a piece of furniture in the next room:

'Is that it?' asked Peyramale.

Father Ollivier tells us that Peyramale questioned Bernadette with 'a bit of uneasiness', as they all stood before the glistening Carrara marble. Peyramale realized only too well that he would not be able to accommodate both the shepherdess and the sculptor. In a letter dated November 30, 1863, he had prepared the sculptor for the ultimate trial:

I seriously doubt that when Bernadette sees your statue, no matter how amazed she may be (sic), she will exclaim: It's her! You won't take offence. . . .

Programmed to be submissive, Bernadette tried to give the desired response:

'That's it . . .'

But she did not know how to pretend. After a moment of silence she continued in a tone of regret, 'almost of pity':

'No, that's not it!' (Memorandum of Ollivier; SEMPÉ, p. 224)

The problem with the statue was the workmanship. According to Bernadette, the characteristics of the Virgin were simplicity, plainness, symmetry, and straightness. The sculptor made her too fancy. He whimsically complicated the folds of her veil and her dress. He bent the head back a bit towards heaven, though Bernadette had insisted that it be straight and erect on her shoulders.

'She raised her eyes, but not her head. He has given her goitre!' protested Bernadette.

The sculptor had added all sorts of slack lines and folds. He had not respected the small size of the apparition; he had taken advantage of the clearing carried out where the rosebush had grown to increase its size. The statue should have been the same height as Bernadette (1 m 40). He had made it 1 m 70 (H 3, pp. 152–156). In addition, he had not respected the youthfulness of the apparition as Bernadette had asked. To her, as to her big sister, Theresa of Avila, the Virgin had seemed 'very much a child'. Or, as George Bernanos put it in his *Diary of a Country Priest*: 'Younger than sin, younger than the race from which she came.'

There is no doubt that the sculptor had been sincere, and that the spark had passed from Bernadette to him. But it had not broken down the conventions which were part and parcel of his academic outlook. 'Art is eloquence,' he had said, when he was formally received into the Lyon Academy. This eloquence betrayed Bernadette.

## A ceremony missed

Neither she nor Dean Peyramale attended the inauguration ceremony for the new statue. The Dean decided that she was to remain at the hospice, so as not to be subjected to the curiosity of admirers at this triumphal ceremony. It is also possible that he did not want an untimely remark from her to prejudice the onlookers' appreciation of the statue.

But Peyramale was subjected to a dose of his own medicine: he too was kept home on April 4, the inauguration day. He was afflicted with a serious illness and his brother, Doctor Peyramale, came down to Lourdes from Momères to be with him. The doctor noted his impoverished state: 'His whole fortune is 45 centimes . . . and there are rents of 35 poor people to pay' at the end of the month, to prevent evictions such as those the Soubirous had experienced (VÉDÈRE, pp. 90–91).

As for the artist, he himself admitted that in this official triumph he experienced 'one of the worst annoyances' in his life as an artist. Viewed from below at an unaccustomed angle, where it was 'lit up by an unforeseen reflection of light', the statue showed 'a complete change in expression'. The artist began to regret the 'polychromy of the ancients', and decided to have the waist-band painted blue.

For Bernadette, however, that day was the day of the big decision which would involve the rest of her life.

*Sister Alexandrine Roques, Superior, with Bernadette (end of 1861—beginning of 1862)*

# 8

# BERNADETTE'S RELIGIOUS VOCATION

On April 4, 1864, after attending Mass in the hospice of
Lourdes, Bernadette looked for the Superior, Sister Alexandrine Roques.

'I now know, dear Mother, which religious order I
should enter.'

'Which one, my child?'

'Yours, dear Mother.'

'Very well, my child, we will talk to the bishop about
this.'

Sister Maria Géraud, who had come to Lourdes for the
inauguration of the new statue, 'was convinced that Bernadette found enlightenment about this decision on her
religious vocation in the Communion she received that
morning' (PONev, 1202 v; D 7, p. 109).

**Long deliberations**

In fact this decision was the fruit of long deliberations,
which she had kept in the dark. The works of Dom Bernard Billet have shed light on the enigmas and apparent
contradictions involved (D 7, pp. 79–128).

A letter of March 8, 1858 (published in D 2) adds new
information. On that day the mayor of Lourdes had a
revealing conversation with Bernadette. He proposed that
she learned the craft of dressmaking or ironing at the

community's expense. Her reply was:

'No, I want to be a nun.'

'But you may change your mind. In the meantime you should learn some trade,' insisted the mayor.

'I won't change my mind. But I do want to do what my mother and father would like me to do' (D 2, p. 149).

Bernadette's first attraction was to the contemplative life, according to the testimony of her two aunts, Bernarde and Basile. She knew about the Carmelite convent in Bagnères. Antoinette Tardhivail, her tutor, had spoken enthusiastically about it as early as the spring of 1858 because it was the great yearning and drama of Antoinette's own life. The latter would have liked to enter that convent, but her health prevented her. She often signed her name as 'Sister Augustine', nostalgically recalling the vocation she could not pursue. Did Bernadette have an opportunity to speak to those nuns through their black curtain or their grill? In any case we do know that she made the acquaintance of a Carmelite friar who had a great reputation for holiness and musical ability: Father Hermann. But Bernadette soon realized that her health would preclude such a choice, even as it had in the case of 'Sister Augustine'. A realist, Bernadette dropped all thoughts which led in that direction. She turned a deaf ear to suggestions from that quarter, even as she did to the suggestions which came from many other convents.

In 1860–1861 she spoke to Jeanne Védère, her cousin, who was the school teacher in Momères, about a religious order named after her patron saint, Bernard. She told Jeanne that she would like to enter it because they practised 'vigils ... fasts ... strict discipline ... mortification'. For a long time it was thought that Bernadette had the Cistercians in mind. But a convent dedicated to Saint Bernard meant the convent of the Bernardines established by Father Cestac in Anglet, near Bayonne. If he had been informed of her wish, the founder would have refused, partly because of Bernadette's health and partly for another reason that he would not give to Bernadette:

'I don't want the world following after her' (D 7, pp. 86–87).

Bernadette does not seem to have ever questioned her desire for a religious vocation, but she did wonder about the possibility of realizing it in practice. Her health was one obstacle, her poverty another. She needed a dowry, and there was no question of asking her family to provide one for her.

According to several witnesses, Bernadette was not attracted to the Sisters of Nevers. But before October 1860, she did in fact have an important conversation about her vocation with Sister Ursule Fardès, the Superior of the hospice. In a later letter Bernadette writes about that conversation in a lyrical tone that is exceptional for her:

> I love to recall the day we were at the wood-house and you spoke to me about my vocation. How often I have thought about that little conversation! I can almost see you sitting on one step of the staircase and me on another. I glance at it every time I go there.... (Letter of June 15, 1866; ESB, p. 190).

But we shall undoubtedly never know what she confided to Sister Fardès on that staircase, any more than we shall know what happened to Nathaniel 'under the fig-tree' (Jn 1:48).

Father Pomian tells us that 'she would have liked the Sisters of the Cross'. He may indeed have tried to point her in that direction, for he was involved with that congregation in the region. However, Bernadette reacted very negatively when these nuns tried to get her to try on the huge head-piece they wore in those days:

'I want nothing to do with this tunnel' (PANev V, 1227).

The Sisters of Saint Vincent de Paul had no more success when they tried the same thing. They invited her to visit when Germaine Raval entered their order.

'I had quite a bad time of it today,' she confided, when

she got back. 'The day seemed awfully long to me. Those nuns tried their habit on me, but I didn't feel at all attracted.'

'Oh, that may mean you will have a vocation, Bernadette!'

'Oh, no! Quite the contrary!' (D 7, p. 89; note 516).

In 1863 the Sisters òf the hospice pointed her in the direction of caring for the sick. It was to be a decisive experience, according to Father Pomian, her confessor:

'She tried her hand at caring for a couple of old people ... fairly disgusting ones. She applied herself to the work with charity and developed a taste for it' (A VII, p. 189).

We know a few details about one of these patients. She was a 'ragged woman, given to drink'. She had 'fallen into a brazier, head first, and was severely burned'.

'From now on you mustn't take so many swigs,' a smiling Bernadette told her (BARBET, 1929 edition, p. 189).

Bernadette confided her attraction to Jeanne Védère:

I love the poor a great deal. I love to take care of sick people. I will stay with the Sisters of Nevers. They gave me a sick person to take care of. When I am well, no one takes care of him except me. I will stay with them. (Letter of September 10, 1879; Védère, p. 71; OG, pp. 192–193)

The problems that held her back were questions of money and her health, and also the feeling of incapacity imbued in her by day-to-day humiliations. In that era people did not take due account of the bad aspects of such an approach.

Bernadette was in this fix when Bishop Forcade of Nevers came to Lourdes on September 27, 1863. He talked to her about her future frankly, as a former missionary to the Far East well might. His adventurous past had taught him simplicity:

'What are you going to be?'

'Nothing, I think.'

'What do you mean, nothing? One certainly must do something here in this world.'

'Well, I am here with the Sisters.'

'Yes, but you are here only for the time being, aren't you?'

'Oh, I will stay here forever.'

'That's easy enough to say, but not so easy to do. Just because they took you in for the time being out of charity, you must not assume that they will let you stay here forever.'

'Why not?'

'Because you are not a nun and you must be one to be admitted into the community once and for all. . . . Here you aren't even a servant. In fact, from today on, you are what you said you were going to be just now: nothing. You won't last anywhere very long on that basis.'

After a brief silence the bishop continued:

'You are no longer a little child. Perhaps you would like to settle down in the world in some suitable occupation?'

'Oh, no, nothing like that!' Bernadette replied vigorously.

'Well, then, why not become a nun? Haven't you ever thought about it?'

'That's impossible. You know very well that I am poor. I would never have the necessary dowry' (FORCADE, pp. 11–12).

The bishop sought to reassure her:

'When we recognize an authentic vocation in poor girls, we do not hesitate to take them in without a dowry.'

'But the girls you take in without a dowry are skilful and clever, so they pay you back. . . . I don't know anything. I am good for nothing.'

'I noticed this very morning that you are good for something.'

'For what?'

'For scraping carrots.'

'Bah! That's not hard,' exclaimed Bernadette with a laugh.

'It doesn't matter. . . . They will certainly find some way

to make use of you, quite apart from the fact that in the novitiate they will be sure to give you much of the training you now lack.'

'Well, in that case I'll think about it; but I haven't really decided yet' (FORCADE, p. 13).

In the following months Bernadette thought about her future on the basis of these new possibilities. Her health went through its usual ups and downs, but it improved during the winter of 1863–1864.

One of the things that Bernadette appreciated in the Sisters of Nevers was their prudent reserve in dealing with her, which she compared with the active solicitation indulged in by some of the other orders of nuns.

'I am going to Nevers because they did not lure me there,' she would say later (PANev 1,547; see PONev 737 and 1110).

Thus her decision of April 4, 1864 was not the result of any sudden inspiration. It was the fruit of long thought.

## Bernadette on holiday (October 4–November 19, 1864)

An unexpected pleasure awaited Bernadette in the autumn of 1864. She went on holiday with her relatives for the first and only time in her life. The idea was thought up by Jeanne Védère, who came to Lourdes with her father. Why not bring Bernadette back with them to Momères? Contrary to expectations, Dean Peyramale gave his permission on the spot. He himself was from Momères, and his brother was a doctor there. Given permission to go for two or three days, Bernadette was to stay there for seven weeks. The very next day Dean Peyramale took a flying trip to Momères and entrusted his brother with the task of transmitting to Bernadette an unlimited 'extension'.

Bernadette did not escape the curiosity that dogged her everywhere. The first few days in Momères she sat in on the class taught by her cousin Jeanne. But her presence attracted the people of the area and class lessons were disturbed. It was better if Bernadette stayed at home. Family life among her cousins delighted her:

> Gay and playful, she greatly enjoyed chatting and bantering with one of her cousins (VÉDÈRE, p. 22; OG, p. 177).

Monsieur Dutour, a publisher in Tarbes, came to Momères. He wanted to get even with his colleague and great rival, Billard-Perrin, who took a good number of photos of Bernadette in 1863. Dutour was doing quite well at selling pictures of Lourdes. In February 1864 he had photographed Bernadette in the hospice and at the grotto. Now he was mounting a full-scale advertising campaign and he wanted to update his stock. He wished to take Bernadette to his studio, and he had already had dealings with the bishop about the matter. He took advantage of Bernadette's availability; he brought her to the Annet studio in Tarbes and took sixteen negatives.

Bernadette was not at all upset by the absence of a regular routine. Her order was within her own self. She was very precise in following her own little personal set of rules:

> She went to Mass every day and received Communion three times a week: Sunday, Wednesday, and Friday. Every day she made her visit to the Blessed Sacrament and said her rosary. When she prayed, one would have said that she was almost in ecstasy, she was so reverent and rapt in meditation (VÉDÈRE, p. 22).

François Soubirous came to visit several times, just as he used to do when his eldest child was staying in Bartrès. It was he who finally decided when she was to return to Lourdes, though she was very happy in Momères. He preferred to see her nearby rather than far away.

The two cousins continued to exchange their thoughts about their respective vocations. This had been going on for some time, and they had discussed the subject at great length by April 4, when Bernadette had made her own decision. Jeanne Védère's religious vocation had been opposed by her family. She had been thinking of the Carmelites, but her father would hear no talk of the cloistered life. Weary of the struggle, Jeanne had resigned herself to a makeshift solution:

'To join the Sisters of St Vincent de Paul with the intention of entering the Carmelites later.'

Bernadette's reply was direct and to the point:

Mind you don't do that! Stay at home instead with your family. That would be almost as if you planned to deceive people and the good God too. . . . But God is not deceived. It is he who gives you the attraction you feel . . . but it is not his idea that you should enter the Sisters of St Vincent de Paul with the intention of going elsewhere later. . . . Be patient, you will succeed (VÉDÈRE, pp. 65 and 68).

In Momères Bernadette is reported to have told her cousin that the biggest difficulty would soon disappear:

This big obstacle was my poor godmother, who was more opposed than anyone else to my entry into the religious life. She was ill at the time. Four days after my cousin left, she died. That was on November 23 (VÉDÈRE, p. 88).

### A request granted

Bernadette had left for Momères without having had any response to her request of April 4. The reason was that in Nevers the Superior General of the religious order, Mother Joséphine Imbert, was hesitant. She was worried that the celebrity of the visionary would mean disturbances for any religious house she might join. But the

Mistress of Novices, Mother Marie Thérèse Vauzo, was in favour of Bernadette's request: sometime later she was to say to the novices:

It will be one of the great good fortunes of my life to see the eyes that have seen the Holy Virgin (PONev 1100 v; ESB, p. 181, no. 48).

The bishop supported the request that he had provoked, accepted and transmitted. So when Bernadette returned to Lourdes on November 19, 1864, she found good news waiting for her. The response was yes.

She broke the news to her parents. She 'made out that she was happy,' noted her brother, Jean-Marie (PONev, 147; D 7, p. 109; also see *Mélanges J. Coppin*, p. 78, note 40, for the correction of the date).

Her postulancy could have begun at once, but Bernadette's health suffered a relapse from the beginning of December to the end of January. She began to get up out of bed only at the beginning of February, according to her letter of February 7, 1865 (D 7, p. 421, no. 1717).

Her convalescence was saddened by the death of Justin Soubirous, the little brother who she used to take to the fields to be breast-fed in the summer of 1856 (D 7, p. 421). He died before he had reached his tenth birthday. The doctors who visited the Soubirous in the unwholesome atmosphere of the Gaol had been right when they said:

If you want to preserve your children, you must not remain here.

## A marriage proposal

On March 5, 1866, someone asked for Bernadette's hand in marriage. The suitor had already expressed his wish on April 20, 1863. His name was Raoul de Tricqueville and

he was studying medicine in Nantes. He directed his proposal to Bishop Laurence as if the latter were the father of
the girl, morally speaking:

> It seems that there is nothing better for me to do than to
> get married, and I would like to marry Bernadette. If I
> am not permitted to marry her, I think I will quit this
> world. I would ask God for the grace to go off and die in
> solitude (D 7, p. 493, no. 1814).

We do not know what Bernadette thought about it, or
even if his letter was conveyed to her. We only know,
thanks to the suitor, that the bishop sent a blunt reply to
his first letter. His request seemed to be contrary 'to what
the Holy Virgin wanted'. But the persistent suitor was to
renew his request during Bernadette's novitiate in Nevers,
sending his appeal to Bishop Forcade (FORCADE, pp.
38–42; L 3, pp. 236–240).

Bernadette began her postulancy in February, 1865. In
April 1866, she drew up her petition to enter the novitiate
(D 7, p. 196).

**A delay**

On April 28, 1866, Bernadette announced her departure
(D 7, p. 498, no. 1822). But Bishop Laurence wanted her
to be in Lourdes for the inauguration of the crypt, the
substructure of the 'chapel' requested by the Virgin Mary.
Sister Alexandrine wrote the following note during this
period:

> Bernadette ... longs for nothing but the moment of
> departure. I fear it will be put off (again) if the Bishop
> of Tarbes demands that she remain here a while longer
> for the sake of the grotto. Pray, dear Mothers, that such
> will not be the case ... so that this child will be
> safeguarded from self-love and from the covetousness

of all the religious orders who come to solicit her, even in our presence. . . . (D 7, p. 499, no. 1823; see p. 78, note 467).

This time Bernadette did attend the ceremony and took part in the first official procession in response to the Virgin Mary's request. It was a joy for her, but it was also the occasion for many affronts.

On May 19, the first day of the triduum, she was dressed in uniform and buried in the ranks of the Children of Mary so that she would not be noticed. On her return Jeanne Védère asked her to come out into the courtyard of the hospice, where people from Momères were waiting to see her. They quickly gathered around her and gave way to exclamations:

'Oh, what a pretty saint!'
'The pretty maid!'
'How happy she is!'

That evening she had to repeat the same performance to get rid of the crowd that was gathering around the hospice and trying to sneak in. It was decided to parade Bernadette so that the people would go away, so she was sent to walk in the cloister for a few moments. The people who managed to get that far tried to touch her and offer her souvenirs.

Jeanne Védère reported what Bernadette told her on that occasion:

How foolish they are! If they want objects touched, let them go to the grotto and leave me in peace (PONev 1234 v).

When Bernadette got safely back inside, she voiced her complaints:

You show me off like some freak (D 7, p. 76, notes 450 and 452).
You parade me like a prize ox (Anastasie Carrière, PANev 909 and PONev, 624).

Finally Bishop Laurence authorized her departure. However, it had been assumed that Bernadette would make the journey with a fellow-postulant, Léontine Mouret. Now the father of the latter girl refused to give his consent. She was scarcely seventeen! They would have to wait. Bernadette wrote to the girl's father on May 26, 1866. Her letter drew tears from his eyes. He permitted their departure (ANDL 42, 1910, p. 311).

## Farewells

Spring 1866 was a time for farewells. Bernadette was brought to Pau where her presence drew so many people that 'the police had to be called in'. On June 25 she went to Tarbes to say goodbye to Bishop Laurence. But he was making his Confirmation rounds and a letter had to suffice. She was also brought to Bagnères because Mother Alexandrine had promised this to the Superior of that house—on the condition that she would be discreet.

Bernadette also said farewell to Jean-Marie Doucet, the sick little boy she had visited on the Piqué farm after the apparitions were over. Since the autumn of 1858 he had been living on the Bourrié farm. He was now fifteen years old. At this very moment he was colouring some engravings of the apparition and some portraits of the visionary for Monsieur Dufour. He was also composing his illustrated memoirs. Bernadette's visits were to be the highlight of his story.

Billard-Perrin came to the hospice to photograph Bernadette with the nuns. He took two photos of her in lay dress, one of her in nun's dress, and another of her with the Children of Mary.

On July 2, two days before Bernadette's departure, Viron got permission from the bishop to do something he had been requesting for a long time. He managed to get three pictures of Bernadette alone. But the snap of her maternal family is blurred, and that of the paternal family is missing. There is no trace of it left.

Viron came to bring the photos himself, wishing to give them to Bernadette as a gift. She refused.

'No, I want to pay for them. If you give them to me, they will not really be mine' (ANDL 42, 1910, p. 311; D 7, p. 125, note 193).

Bernadette gave the photos to her friends. She also distributed all the little objects that still remained in her wardrobe at the hospice. Then she made her last visit to the grotto. It cost her dearly, but there was none of the excessive drama we find in certain accounts of the scene. Aunt Basile Castérot, who shared the final evening with Bernadette and saw her the morning of the day before her departure, strikes just the right note:

> I was not there when she went to the grotto for the last time. I know that she suffered in leaving it, but she put on a brave front (PONev, 810 v).

On the evening of July 3, the whole family got together at the Lacadé mill for the farewell meal. It was 11:00 p.m. before they broke up, an unusual hour in those days:

> A large crowd was waiting for Bernadette outside our door; and when she went out, everyone pressed around her ... to touch her (Anne-Marie Lamathe, proprietor of the mill, PATarbes, p. 315).

The next morning her closest relatives went to the hospice for the final farewells. The group included Bernadette's father, her mother—'already ill' (A VII, p. 287, no. 556), Aunt Bernarde, and Aunt Basile.

Bernadette was wearing a blue dress, a gift that was forced upon her 'by the Superior of the hospice'. The things she was taking with her were in a coarse linen bag of multicoloured stripes. Her trousseau was jammed into a bulging trunk; in those days a prospective bride or nun brought a lifetime of linen with her. At least that was what was done by those who could afford it: i.e., the middle classes and religious orders. Bernard, Bernadette's youngest brother, who was now six, describes the scene:

> All of us cried. I did what the others did, not really knowing the reason for these tears (PONev 4, 831; D 7, p. 126, note 698).

'We cried, but she did not,' specifies Aunt Basile. Bernadette herself said:

> You are dears to cry. I can't stay here forever (PONev, 810 v).

### Lourdes is left behind

In Tarbes they met the Superior of Bagnères and her postulant, Marie Larrotis. Aunt Bernarde, Toinette, and Sister Victorine, who accompanied Bernadette that far, remained on the platform with a group of friends and inquisitive people. Lourdes and its mountains faded away in the blue horizon amid a plume of smoke. That was the next-to-last farewell.

The final farewell took place in Andrest (near Vic), where the Mouret family owned some property. Monsieur Mouret thus managed to prolong his final moments with his daughter Léontine for a bit longer. It had cost him a great deal to part with her:

> A crowd of friends has come. . . . They express a burning desire to see Bernadette. To satisfy them, Bernadette comes to the door of the coach. But the whistle is already sounding, and it is time to depart. There are tearful embraces and farewells. The train disappears, carrying the future nuns towards Nevers (ANDL 42, 1910, pp. 308–309).

*Below: the habit is tried on Bernadette*

# 2

# NEVERS
(July 7, 1866–April 16, 1879)

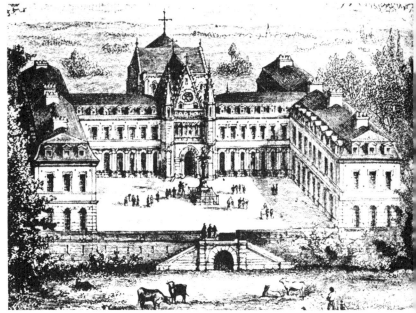

*The Saint-Gildard Convent in Nevers*

# 9

# THE NOVITIATE

## The trip (July 4–7, 1866)

For the first and last time Bernadette boarded a train and left her native Pyrenees. Her keen senses took in all the new sights she saw. To her friends in Lourdes she wrote:

Let me tell you about our trip. We arrived in Bordeaux at 6:00 p.m. on Wednesday, July 4. We stayed there until 1:00 p.m. on Friday. You can rest assured that we made good use of the time to go sightseeing. And in a coach, if you please! They took us around to visit all the houses of our congregation in Bordeaux. I assure you that they are not like the one in Lourdes. The main one, in particular, is more like a palace than a religious house.

We went to see the Carmelite church. Then we headed for the Garonne River to see the boats. We also went to the Botanical Gardens. There I saw something new. Can you guess what? Fish of all colours: red, black, white, and grey! I think the nicest thing of all was to see those little creatures swimming around under the gaze of all those children.

Bernadette, with a sympathy that was wholly Francis-can, recognized herself in those little fishes. Like them, she was an animal on display. Now, if she had her way, she would abandon that role once and for all.

On July 6 they reached the second stop on their journey: Périgueux. They left there the next morning at 7:00 a.m. and arrived in the Nevers station that evening at 10:30 p.m. A coach was waiting for the two superiors and the three postulants: Marie, Léontine, and Bernadette. They lay down to sleep in the huge, silent house. Bernadette could only imagine what the figures shrouded in darkness might really be like.

## The apparitions recounted

At 1:00 p.m. the next day—Sunday, July 8—all the novices and postulants were summoned to the novitiate hall. All the nuns of the community, as well as nuns from two other convents in Nevers, had been invited. For the first and last time Bernadette was to tell the story of the apparitions to them, before burying herself in the silence that she so ardently sought.

To make clear the break between this last public witness and the reserve of the religious life that she was about to enter, Bernadette was permitted to wear the peasant dress that had become famous through the photos which were being sold to the public. In particular, she was allowed to wear her white hood.

The mistress of novices presided, alongside the superiors who had come from the Pyrenees. Three hundred nuns had gathered—the nuns of the motherhouse plus other nuns from the town and the surrounding area. The mistress of novices introduced the visionary but in somewhat less than flattering terms. She was anxious to preserve Bernadette's humility. Bernadette began to speak hesitantly, first in *patois* and then in standard French. She resorted to *patois* first almost automatically, as if to protect herself, following the outline of events that she had recounted so many times now:

The first time I went to the grotto was Thursday, February 11. I went with two other girls to gather wood. When we reached the mill, I asked them if they would like to go see where the canal water joined up with the Gave. They said yes. So we followed the water of the canal and found ourselves in front of the grotto, unable to go any farther ...

Then she described the gust of wind and the appearance of the lady in a white dress with a blue waist-band. When Bernadette got to the muddy water of February 25 and told how she rejected it three times, Mother Alexandrine Roques, the Superior from Lourdes, spoke out emphatically:

'You can judge from that how little mortified she was.'

Picking up the point, Mother Marie-Thérèse Vauzou chided Bernadette amiably: 'You were not mortified, Bernadette.'

'Well, the water was very dirty' (L 3, Vol. 1, p. 60).

Mother Vauzou didn't like the idea of Bernadette having secrets, even if they came from the Blessed Virgin. She liked transparency in her novices. But she got no further information from Bernadette.

Finally, Bernadette had to tell the audience about her vocation. She was asked to describe all the head-pieces that were tried on her by other congregations of nuns.

'There was even one that bore the name of the Immaculate,' she noted.

'Our congregation was one of the very first to be dedicated to the Immaculate Conception,' said Mother Marie-Thérèse Vauzou pointedly.

After telling her story Bernadette donned the pleated little cap and cloak of the postulant. At Vespers inquisitive eyes would have a hard time identifying her among the other forty-two postulants. Bernadette formally declared that she had come to 'hide herself', and her superiors had exactly the same idea in mind. But the frequent calls at the main door of the convent made it clear that this was to be no easy thing to do.

**Homesickness**

As was customary, Bernadette was entrusted to a 'guardian angel': another novice who was to help her to get used to her new life. Her guardian angel was Sister Emilienne Duboé. Bernadette felt homesick, as she was to admit later to help Valentine Borot with the same problem:

> I was quite upset at the start. When I got a letter from home, I would wait until I was alone to open it because I felt I couldn't read it without crying out all my tears (L 453).

She overcame her feelings of uprootedness not only with courage but also with humour. To Lourdes she wrote:

> I must tell you that Léontine and I passed Sunday watering the day well with our tears! The good Sisters encourage us at it, saying that it was the sign of a solid vocation (ESB, p. 241).

Bernadette mobilized all her resources to get acclimatized; they included the following symbolic game reported by Sister Philomène:

> She collected three stones in the courtyard of the novitiate. 'Here are the companions of mine that I love,' she said, showing them to us. On the first she had written 'Lourdes' on the second 'the grotto', and on the third 'Nevers, Mother-house' (L 17).

Her consolation was to visit the statue of Our Lady of the Waters at the back of the garden, in 'a kind of grotto', as she wrote to the Sisters in Lourdes:

> It was there I could unburden my heart the first few days. Later our dear Mistress deigned to let us go there every day.

It was not really that Bernadette found any 'resemblance' there, as some have tried to intimate. Rather, it was the open air of the place that brought back to her mind the grotto, the gesture of welcome, and a certain smile. The uprooting was hard on Bernadette. She had never before left her region, her mountains, and the human atmosphere of the Bigorre province. She was attached in countless ways to those places where grace had blossomed for her.

She admitted that it was 'a great sacrifice' (L 375), indeed 'the greatest sacrifice' of her life (L 754). But she shouldered this new stage in her life without reservations:

My mission in Lourdes is finished (L 391).
Lourdes is not heaven (L 759).

**Taking the habit**

With forty-two other postulants Bernadette donned her religious habit on July 29, three weeks after her arrival. She abandoned her little cap for the head-piece with two white strips jutting down diagonally from under the chin. The exchange occurred during the ceremony itself. The postulants disappeared into the sacristy and came back out with a white bridal veil on their head. Bishop Forcade then replaced it with a black veil, saying:

You are going to receive a new name, which will remind you that you are separated from the world. You belong to Jesus Christ whom you wish to choose as your spouse.

For the first time the bishop gave Bernadette her new name as a nun, saying:

Sister Marie-Bernard, may the Lord clothe you with the new human being created in God's image, in justice and holiness born of truth (Eph 4:24).

The mistress of novices let her keep the name of her patron saint in Baptism, Bernard of Clairvaux, but she added the patronage of Mary. As she explained:

It was altogether fitting that I give her the name of the holy Virgin, whose child she is (RC, p. 30).

After taking their habit, the novices were scattered all over France. They would complete their formation in the field, working in each of the houses to which they were sent. It was a sound formula, which associated the grass-roots communities with the development of the young aspirants. It continued until it was prohibited by the Congregation for Religious.

### An exceptional case

Bernadette, however, was kept at the mother-house. Her superiors decided that it would be easier to protect her in that fortress than in any hospital or school, open to all and sundry, where she might again become the prey of curiosity-seekers.

Being treated as an exception was something that weighed heavily on Bernadette. She acknowledged as much when she tried to console Sister Emilienne Duboé, who was disappointed at being assigned to Clermont-Ferrand:

How happy I would be if I could go somewhere to work instead of being obliged to stay here and do nothing! (L 24)

She appreciated the uniform that protected her from the inquisitive, particularly the veil that allowed her to hide herself. She liked to pull it over herself and bury herself in it during her thanksgiving. But the novitate did not foster complaisance. When Mother Vauzou made a remark about it to her, Bernadette replied:

It's my little house (L 28).

Who can blame her? Didn't she come there to hide herself? (L 29).

## A death-bed profession

Around August 16, 1866, Bernadette entered the infirmary; but it was only a case of fatigue. In September, however, her asthma was much worse. She was confined to bed, no longer permitted 'to go downstairs' (L 33). Sister Émilie, the assistant infirmarian, was disturbed to see her 'choking' without uttering a word of complaint.

'It's as it should be, it's nothing,' Bernadette told her (L 41).

As a precaution, someone kept watch over her during the night, as people had more than once when she was in Lourdes. Bernadette's chief concern was that her attendant get some sleep.

'Take a rest in that arm-chair,' she told Sister Eléonore. 'I'll call you when I need you' (L 34).

Her detachment was complete and unreserved: 'The good God sent this to me; I must accept it' (L 35). Confused by all the care and attention she was getting, she remarked: 'The poor are not treated like this' (L 50).

It was not that Bernadette was completely indifferent and had no desires of her own. At first she was happy when she was sent her companion in the novitiate, Léontine Mouret, to help out in the infirmary. The infirmarian made this choice deliberately. But soon another novice appeared in the infirmary in her place.

'Is Léontine sick?' asked Bernadette.

'No, but the mistress of novices has forbidden me to pick her.'

'Ah, I understand,' replied Bernadette (L 48).

She could not hide how painful it was for her to eat. When Sister Émilie Marcillac brought in her breakfast plate, Bernadette told her:

'It's my penance you're bringing me.'

But she would take it without saying a word (L 42). In her suffering she would look at the crucifix with an expression 'that spoke volumes' (B 2, p. 36).

When she was feeling better, she would laugh and tease and even 'sing a few verses in her Pyrenees dialect'.

'She would laugh heartily when she noticed that I didn't understand a word of it,' recounts Sister Émile (L 44).

Bernadette accepted the joy with the pain, saying: 'All that is good for heaven' (L 46).

On October 25, her condition grew graver. They lighted candles before the statue of the Blessed Virgin. Robert Saint-Cyr, the physician of the community, assured them that she would not last the night. Sister Marcelline, who shared her room, was transferred to a room next-door. Mother Marie-Thérèse prepared Bernadette for death. The chaplain, Father Victor Douce, administered Extreme Unction to her.

Since Bernadette was going to leave this world, it was proper that she should make her religious profession on the point of death. That required a dispensation from the bishop, but he was out making his rounds. When he got back at 7:00 p.m., he hastened to the scene in person: 'I don't want to give up the honour of receiving her profession to anyone else.'

The bishop himself offered the following account of the whole scene:

> I found the sick girl out of breath, not to say gasping her last. She had just vomited a small basin-full of blood, and the basin was still there by her bed. I went up to her:
>
> 'You are going to die, my dear child, and I have been told that you wish to make your profession. I'm here to receive it.'

'I can't pronounce the formula: no strength' (Bernadette in a faint voice).

'That's no problem. I will pronounce the words for you. You need only respond.'

It was with the poverty of a simple Amen that Bernadette professed the vows that would link her once and for all to God in the Congregation of the Sisters of Charity. The bishop continues:

The Superior General ... remained at the foot of the bed with the pious intention of closing Bernadette's eyes. I had hardly gone out of the room when the dying victim found her tongue again, smiled at her Superior, and said:

'You have had me make my profession because you thought I was going to die tonight. Well, I will not die tonight.'

There has been much comment and debate about the rebuke which Mother Joséphine, the Superior General, was supposed to have dished out to Bernadette at this point. Here is Bishop Forcade's account of it:

'What! You knew that you were not supposed to die tonight, and you did not tell me that? So you make the bishop come here at this ungodly hour and get us all in an uproar over you! You're nothing but a little fool! I'm telling you that if you are not dead tomorrow morning, I'm going to take away your veil of religious profession ... And I'll send you back to the novitiate with the simple novice's veil ...'

'As you see fit, my dear Mother.'

Undoubtedly the bishop injected a note of harshness into the conversation, which he did not witness directly. One should assume a tone of humour in it and not take it too seriously as a threat. There is clear proof of this in the fact that Bernadette kept the insignia of her profession and showed them to her novitiate companions with an air of peace and joy.

'Thief!' Sister Charles Ramillon said to her, looking at the veil and the crucifix lying on her bed.

'Thief or not,' said Bernadette, 'now they are mine. I have them, I belong to the congregation, and they cannot send me away' (L 54).

Although recovery from an illness nullifies a death-bed profession according to the provisions of church law, the community hesitated to enforce this provision insofar as Bernadette was concerned. From the second month of her novitiate on, she had been ill constantly. They did not want to deprive her of the beneficent security she now enjoyed.

'I've got it. . . . It's mine,' she would say, showing the crucifix received at her profession to others.

'The good God didn't want me,' she said to Sister Émilie. 'I went right up to the gate and he told me: "Go away. It's too soon" ' (L 53).

She told Sister Louise: 'I am still too bad. The good God didn't want me' (L 53).

But God did want her mother. Louise Soubirous died on December 8, 1866, during the Vespers of the Immaculate Conception. Forty-one years old, she had been used up by hard work, poverty, and nine childbirths, of which only four children were left.

'I could not express to you the pain that I have suffered,' wrote Bernadette to Father Pomian. 'I learned about her death sooner than I learned about her illness' (L 55).

## A time of testing

Bernadette was well on February 2, 1867. She returned to the novitiate. Mother Marie-Thérèse Vauzou got hold of her to make up for lost time.

'Well now, Sister Marie-Bernard, we are going to get into the time of your testing.'

'Oh, Mother, I pray you will not go too quickly' (L 69), replied the prudent Bernadette with a smile.

According to Sister Léontine Villaret, Mother Vauzou was also supposed to have said: 'Now we are going to come down on you.'

'I hope you will do it gently,' Bernadette is supposed to have replied.

This response did not 'edify' Mother Vauzou, Sister Léontine assures us.

Bernadette's novitiate companions bear abundant witness to her sober and solid piety:

> Nothing distinguished her from the others except her regularity, her preciseness, her silence and, above all, her extreme charity. . . . (Sister Joseph Caldairou; RC, pp. 71–72).

As for the tests and trials about which she was warned, the ones reported to us hardly go beyond playful teasing. Sister Stanislas recounts the following incident:

> One day, while the rule was being read to the novices, Sister Marie-Bernard was sitting on a step next to the mistress of novices and mending the latter's apron. One passage in the reading dealt with the apparition of the Blessed Virgin to a shepherdess. At that point Mother Marie-Thérèse Vauzou turned to Sister Marie-Bernard and said: 'That's how the holy Virgin always deals with shepherdesses, isn't it, Sister Marie-Bernard?'
>
> 'Yes, my dear Sister,' Bernadette replied amiably (L 91).

Another day there was a little raffle of a statue of St Germaine Cousin for the novices. Bernadette won. Mother Vauzou is said to have made the following comment 'in an ironic vein'.

'A shepherdess can't help falling into the hands of a shepherdess' (testimony of Sister Isabelle; L, 91).

Still another day Sister Marie-Bernard was waiting for

her instruction time 'at the door of the mistress of novices'. Sister Marguerite thought she detected a certain amount of fear in Bernadette (L 13). But Bernadette did not seem to be affected 'when Mother Vauzou dismissed her' for her 'fits of coughing' (RC, p. 83).

Other bits of testimony stress the happy side of their relationship. According to Justine Pelat, 'she seemed content ... when the main hall of the novitiate had been made ready to receive Mother Marie-Thérèse. Ah, then you could see her overflowing happiness sparkling. The maternal air of our venerated mistress seemed to want to draw all our hearts to herself and enfold them in her bosom' (B 2, p. 51).

'One day when the mistress was returning home from a trip,' recounts Sister Stanislas, 'we were waiting for her in the cloister. . . . When she arrived, Sister Marie-Bernard rushed into her arms as might a child deprived of its mother for a long time. Sister Molinery (Mistress of Studies for the novitiate) said to Bernadette: "Well, well, Sister Marie-Bernard. What enthusiasm on seeing your mistress again!"

' "Oh yes, my dear Sister," replied Bernadette. "It was much too natural ... I have repented of it" ' (L 90).

These texts must be situated in the context of nineteenth-century religious life. The novices often came at a young age and from a very protected home environment. They were inexperienced and they had not been separated before from the protective presence of their own mother, in whose shadow they had lived. A transfer of this maternal function had to take place in the convent. And the maternity of the religious superior was all the more important because it was a collective and sacred maternity.

In this atmosphere a basic differentiation took place. Many young nuns found peace and equilibrium by following the path of spiritual childhood. The strong personalities, who stood out as the bulwarks of tradition and the guiding spirits of the community, found a higher equilibrium in exercising the responsibilities of spiritual motherhood. The most famous model of this type is Theresa of Avila. Unlike women in the world at that time, who for the most part were restricted to the home and to passivity, these women had to make decisions, be creative, govern, and travel.

The most difficult position was that of strong personalities who, for a variety of reasons, never gained access to these maternal functions and suffered from the non-fulfilment of their human potential. On the human level this was undoubtedly the case with Bernadette. Endowed with qualities that would have enabled her to exercise serious responsibility, she found that her exceptional status kept her in a 'protected' situation. She suffered from not fulfilling her human potential. And that helps to explain why she died young.

The real trials of this period were the visits which Bernadette could not be completely spared, even though she had come there to hide herself away. How could the community refuse audiences to bishops, to members of the pontifical curia, to important benefactors, or to Henri Lasserre, who was preparing his *Histoire des apparitions* at the request of the Bishop of Tarbes? If they wanted to come off well when major requests were made, what could they do but give their visitors the satisfaction of 'seeing' Bernadette at least. To this end they would give Bernadette odd assignments so that she would have to walk past some area where the visitor might view her from a hidden vantage point. Bernadette herself was not fooled by all this. And since her orders were simply to deliver some message or object, she would often evade the visitor by taking a route different from her usual one.

On the other hand Bernadette did not seem to understand the connection between her presence in the infirmary and the fact that the bishop himself would come to hear the sacrament of Penance.

'How odd that a bishop should put himself to the trouble of hearing the Confession of sick Sisters,' was her only comment (L 107).

**Bernadette's blunders**

During this period Bernadette's gaiety got her over the trials and tests. She had a ready laugh and her 'blunders' as a novice give her many occasions to exercise it.

One day she was sent to get hot water in the kitchen. There was no one there. She got the water herself. In came Sister Cécile, the cook, who was a 'fairly rigid' woman.

'You should have asked for permission! Put that water back where you got it from!' (L 486) exclaimed Sister Cécile.

The idea of 'putting water back in the tap' delighted Bernadette. Her humour completely disarmed Sister Cécile.

'There was that little snip of a nun laughing. A bigger one would have bawled her eyes out' (L 486).

Bernadette suggested to Louise Brusson that they should 'teach a lesson' to a postulant who 'often used to look at herself in the mirror of a little chest in the linen-room'.

'Write something to her on the mirror,' suggested Bernadette.

'I got paper and pencil,' recounted Sister Louise, 'and I wrote: "Better look at your soul".'

This initiative was beyond the proper functions of the two novices. Mother Vauzou demanded to know who the culprits were. Bernadette was the first to confess.

Another day they were in the refectory eating the hard circles of chopped carrots. Bernadette came down on them a bit too vigorously with her fork and the carrots went 'rolling the length of the table'. The laughter was so contagious that 'we couldn't eat any more', reports Sister Louise:

> At the end of the meal, Sister Marie-Bernard turned to me and said: 'Let's go!'
> I knew what she meant. So we headed off to confess our fault to our mistress of novices (L 86).

On another occasion, according to Sister Madeleine, Bernadette was given the task of mending a head-piece 'torn from one end to the other'. She confided her troubles to the infirmarian.

'I will never be able to mend this head-piece.'

'Don't worry,' replied Sister Madeleine. 'I've got some pieces of material that are not in such bad shape. I'll give you one of them.'

But the nun in charge of that work was not pleased and her rebuke was 'severe':

'That's not the one I gave you!'

In the novitiate it did not do to favour intelligence over obedience. When Sister Madeleine tried to offer an excuse for her, Bernadette replied simply:

'I was in the wrong. I did not bring back the head-piece that had been given to me' (L 189).

However, Bernadette had no liking for those patching jobs, nor for the really worn-out vestments that somehow fell to her to mend.

'Look, all they give me are pieces fit for the junk-pile!' she said to Sister Elizabeth.

'Oh, your virtue doesn't go beyond that!'

Bernadette never assumed the statue-like pose rather expected of a visionary. When she arrived at the convent, she astonished the nuns with the question:

'Do they skip with a rope in the novitiate?'

On being told no, she explained simply:

'It's just that I love to turn the rope for the others' (L 14).

During one recreation period, the sister in the kitchen challenged her teasingly to 'drink an egg' that had been freshly laid. Before Bernadette had time to reflect, the two ends of the egg had been pierced with a needle and she downed the egg. But right away she reconsidered the matter.

'Now I must go find the Assistant Mother and ask her for permission!' (L 370).

And she did.

Bernadette also had to laugh at the photos of her which

*Bernadette as a nun*

were now on sale for ten cents. The price has gone down.
She also laughed about her short stature. It gave her an
opportunity to cheer up her companion in the row, Sister
Joseph Caldairou, who was one centimetre taller than herself. They had fun making themselves taller and shorter,
like two clowns in a circus. Bernadette had no complex
about being short. Was this perhaps because the Virgin
appeared to her in humble guise and seemed to be about
her height?

Bernadette had a taste for the picturesque, a gift for
repartee, and a modest estimation of her own person. One
day the person who was to give some word of edification,
as provided by the rule, was absent. The others urged
Bernadette to speak instead.

'I do not know what to say. I am a stone. How can you
squeeze anything out of a stone?' (L 81)

Anyway, this humble response was uttered in such a
way that Sister Stéphane Vareillaud never forgot it.

On May 16, 1867, Antoinette Dalias arrived in Nevers
from Gers. She was eighteen years old. She was to become
Sister Bernard and one of Bernadette's many friends. The
beginning of their friendship was almost comical. On May
19, the new arrival was talking to Sister Berganot.

'I have been here three days, and no one has shown
Bernadette to me yet!'

'Bernadette? But there she is!' replied Sister Berganot,
pointing to the girl next to her.

'This one here!' exclaimed Sister Bernard, who had formed a 'more elaborate idea' of the visionary.

'But of course, Mademoiselle, just this one here,' replied Bernadette amiably. She was to show real fellow-feeling for Antoinette from that moment on (L 72).

*Bishop Forcade*

*Novitiate hall where Bernadette received her assignment*

# 10

# RELIGIOUS PROFESSION
# (OCTOBER 30, 1867)

On October 30, 1867, Bernadette made her religious profession, her hands enfolded between those of Bishop Forcade. Sister Bernard Dalias tells us that her voice was 'firm and without affectation'. Sister Véronique, however, reports that it 'quivered a little'. She committed herself for life to practice the vows of 'poverty, chastity, obedience, and charity'.

The fourth and last vow was established in 1682 by Dom de Laveyne, the founder of the congregation. It was suppressed a little later, however, when Rome reviewed and revised the religious constitutions in accordance with the norms of canon law. Charity does not lend itself to canonical forms.

## No assignment for Bernadette

In the afternoon of the same day each professed nun received what was customarily called 'an obedience': that is, an assignment in some convent. Bishop Forcade himself presided over the ceremony in the novitiate hall. Bernadette's 43 companions were called, one after the other. They were given a crucifix, a book containing the constitutions of the order, and their letter of obedience (FORCADE, p. 32).

It now seems that the bishop had finished. Had he forgotten Bernadette? She leant towards her neighbour, Sister Anastasie:

'They give one to everyone ... I would have really liked to do as everyone does' (PONev 624–625).

Now Bishop Forcade turned to the Mother General:

'And Sister Marie-Bernard?'

'Your Excellency, she is good for nothing.'

Mother Joséphine said this, 'smiling', pointing out Sister Caldairou, and in a low voice that could only be heard in the front rows (PONev 1297 v).

When Bernadette approached, the bishop said—this time out loud:

'Sister Marie-Bernard, nowhere!' (PONev 533 v).

Then he spoke directly to Bernadette.

'Is it true, Sister Marie-Bernard, that you are good for nothing?'

'Yes, it's true.'

'Well then, my poor child, what are we going to do with you?'

'Well, I told you that in Lourdes when you wanted to get me to enter the community, and you replied that it would not matter' (FORCADE, p. 32–33).

At this point the Superior General intervened, as had been pre-arranged:

'If you will, Your Excellency, we could keep her out of charity here in the mother-house and give her some sort of work in the infirmary, even if it be only to clean up and prepare beverages for the sick. Since she is always ill, it would be right up her street.'

## The job of prayer

The bishop agreed and turned to Bernadette.

'I will try,' she replied.

The bishop assumed a graver air and spoke out solemnly:

*The Saint-Gildard infirmary with the pots used by Bernadette*

'I give you the job of prayer' (PONev 1297 v).

The whole scene had been carefully planned and staged to resolve the following problem of conscience. They did not want to send Bernadette to a convent where she would be exposed to 'the curiosity of the public'. But the tasks in the mother-house were regarded as the 'top jobs in the congregation'. Only in an exceptional case would newly professed nuns be assigned there. So they decided to give the outward trappings of humiliation to an assignment that might otherwise have seemed to be a crowning honour. This is how Bishop Forcade himself explained the scene to Count Lafond.

In the recreation that followed, Bernadette did not show her wound. Her deeper sentiments could be glimpsed in the encouragement she would give a bit later on to one of her first sick patients, Louise Brusson. The latter was confined to bed in the infirmary for bronchitis, and she was 'suffering a great deal from the mustard plasters and the vesicants'.

'Come on, my big Augustine,' said Bernadette, 'it's for the good God. We must suffer for him. He suffered enough for us' (L 116).

# 11

# BERNADETTE AS INFIRMARIAN
## (OCTOBER 30, 1867—JUNE 1873)

Now Bernadette was the assistant infirmarian, entrusted with all sorts of small jobs. They ranged from taking care of the flower-pots for the Blessed Virgin to taking care of the night pots of the patients. She was used to the job because she had been assigned to cleaning the toilets during her novitiate. It posed no problems for her.

**Taking charge**

She had a knack for the job of infirmarian, as she had found out earlier in Lourdes. Sister Marthe, the infirmarian, was amazed to see how this little snip of a nun could take charge of patients. A little 'shh!' from her was enough to restore silence (L 136). A single epithet, 'Wastrel!' was enough to shut up Sister Pélagie, who had a hard time controlling her tongue (L 137).

Her humour and air of authority created a good atmosphere in the infirmary. She knew how to empathize with her patients without going too far. To Sister Bernard Dalias, compatriot from Gers whom she addressed with the familiar 'tu' form, she said:

'My poor Bernard, you can't take any more. You are half done in.'

To Sister Dominique Brunet, who was excessively worried about a prospective dental operation, she said:

'Mademoiselle, do you mean to tell me that you do not want suffering?' (L 155).

Bernadette's arrival was right on time. Sister Marthe, the infirmarian, was ill herself. More and more her work was becoming too much for her. On April 12, 1870, she was sent away for a rest. The infirmary did not suffer from her absence. Bernadette was on hand to take charge of things, and all went well.

The infirmarian returned on July 9, worse off than when she left. On December 23, her condition worsened. The next year, March 22, the bishop came to visit her. It was a sign that her condition was desperate. She died on November 8, 1872.

**Chief infirmarian**

Without any fuss, Sister Marie-Bernard had assumed all the work and responsibility. She had no official title or assignment, but she was in fact the chief infirmarian of the mother-house.

She took pains to learn her job well, including how to convert from one set of measurements to another. On her infirmary notes she wrote out some of the more difficult conversions that are no longer familiar today:

1 grain equals 5 centigrams
3 scruples or 1 gros equals 4 grams
1 ounce equals 32 grams

She stressed the importance of these calculations:

Since a change in the position of the comma (French uses a comma in measurements where English uses a period: e.g., 1,32 instead of 1.32) may make a very big difference, it is very desirable that in the various formulas the amounts in grams, decigrams, centigrams, and milligrams be written out completely (ESB, p. 311).

To avoid any mistake, Bernadette wrote down the quantities in both measurements on the formula sheets she prepared for various illnesses: e.g., spitting of blood, dysentery, and scrofula. Here is her chart for the treatment of rheumatism of the joints:

3 cups, infusion of elder.
Add to each 5 drops of aconite extract.
Aconitine liniment: 18 grains ... 1 gram.
Olive oil: 36 grains, 2 grams.
Hog's lard: 1 ounce, 32 grams (ESB, p. 312).

She had a sharp eye and initiative. When she noticed that Sister Angèle's chapped hands were bleeding, she said:

'You shame me with those hands. You must come to the infirmary, and I will take care of you.'

'Up there,' reported Sister Angèle, 'she put honey on my hands, and a few days later I was fine' (L 161).

It was undoubtedly honey from the beeswax comb. She also treated Sister Angèle's eyes. And since the eye-wash made her cry, Bernadette said:

'What! I give you one drop and you give me several of them ...' (L 164)

She insisted on the observance of the rule with a sense of conviction that was a bit rigid, as was usual in those days, but she also used tact. The patients confided in her, telling her not only their difficulties but even their dreams. Her interpretation of dreams was not grounded on Freud or astrology, but it indicated sound psychological intuition. Sister Julienne Capmartin had been deeply troubled by a dream in which the child Jesus indicated some dissatisfaction with her. On this foundation Bernadette intuited a somewhat disordered affection for one of her companions. The point struck home to Sister Julienne (L 311).

The same Sister Julienne used to read her Children of Mary book in bed, even though she had been advised to stay wrapped up under the covers so as to perspire.

'So look there, a fervour woven of disobedience!' remarked Bernadette. The book disappeared (L 313).

Sister Eudoxie tried to leave the infirmary without permission and go back downstairs. Bernadette made clear her disapproval in such pointed terms that the would-be free spirit was stopped in her tracks:

'What am I supposed to do?'

'Get back in bed and lie down! Sacrifice is worth more than prayer.'

The next morning the patient was permitted to get up and to go back to the novitiate (L 305 c).

If she applied the rule strictly to others, she did so to herself as well. One winter day Bernadette found the infirmary too warm because the heaters were too hot, so she opened the windows. The Superior General entered, was shocked to find the windows open, and severely rebuked Bernadette.

'Aren't you ashamed of yourself for doing that?'

'Oh no, my dear Mother!'

But a few moments later Bernadette 'closed the windows and, fifteen minutes after that, went down to the community to confess her fault' (L 282).

## Daily life in the infirmary

Bernadette's day in the infirmary usually began at 7:45 a.m., according to Sister Eudoxie Chatelain. First she checked the condition of the patients and served them the breakfast that was brought to them from the kitchen. She would move from one section of the infirmary to the next; she had no time to sit down herself. Now and then she would offer a pious word of encouragement to the patients:

'Love the good God truly, my children, that is everything' (L 304).

She was not reluctant to watch over the sick or to get up in the middle of the night to assist the temporary helpers assigned to her. Sister Clémence Chassan, who was trained in the work by Bernadette, testified that she had awakened Bernadette several times (B 2, 117–118). Bernadette told her in confidence:

'I would love to take care of the sick in the hospices. I'm afraid my health is the reason that I have not been sent there. But I submit to the will of God. Let him do with me what he wills.'

## The alarms of 1869

The bad side of her life was the ups and downs of her own health. In 1869 she celebrated Easter in bed. According to her letter of April 6, 1869 (RSL, no. 21, 1968, p. 25), it was a 'violent crisis,' but it did not last 'long'.

In October of that year she was confined to bed again. Sister Cécile Pagès, who had been appointed to the infirmary in Paris, had to remain at the mother-house. She gives us the following details:

Bernadette at the time was in bed, spitting up whole basins of blood. I applied some vesicants to her. She said: 'You can raise blisters all you want. I am as hardened to pain as cats are.'

Things were going so badly that the subject of death was considered:

'If one sacrifices one's life truly, won't one go to heaven?' Bernadette asked me in the presence of Mother Joséphine Imbert, the Superior General.

I replied gaily: 'At least we would have one saint, for there is none in the congregation.'

Our venerable Mother replied: 'You think there is none? Well, I think there are.'

'But not canonized!' I replied.

On leaving the room, the substitute infirmarian expressed her worry to the Superior General:

'The doctor says that she could die in a fit of spitting blood.'

## Scholarly disputes

Bernadette was up and on her feet on October 13, 1869, in order to give testimony on a delicate matter. The chaplains of Lourdes have begun to publish a little history of the apparitions in the *Annales*. Public demand had prompted them to take this course because the history being written by Henri Lasserre was slow in coming out. The popular and familiar tone of the little history greatly upset the writer, whose aim was to present a formal and dignified account. Lasserre hastened to Nevers to get Bernadette's criticisms of the little history, so that he might wield them against his rivals. He recorded her every least word of astonishment and denial, drew up a document in legal form, and had her sign it.

On November 16, Father Sempé, the chief chaplain, came to Nevers to defend the work of the chaplains. Now Bernadette was subjected to pleas from the other side. Insofar as the history of Lourdes itself was concerned, the arguments dealt only with minute details, which I have treated in another work (see B 2, pp. 79–107). In the end they contributed very little to the full historical story of the apparitions. But Bernadette now discovered all the human argument that was to surround the great event of her life. She also came to realize how much she herself had forgotten. The experience made a deep, almost traumatic, impression on her. She realized that her every word would be wielded by one side or another in a dispute which did not matter to her at all. Her memory of the apparitions began to grow blurred, just as the message about the procession had slipped her mind under Peyramale's savage reception on March 2, 1858.

## Alarms of death and war (1870)

On April 12, 1870, the two infirmarians were confined to bed at the same time. Bernadette's condition again seemed grave. Sister Honorine Laffarge gives us her impression:

> I went into the infirmary and I found this dear Sister in her death-agony, so to speak. It seemed to me that she had no more than a few hours to live.
> 'My dear Sister,' I said to her, 'our Mistress has sent me to find out how you spent the night?'
> 'Tell her not to worry herself. I will not die today!' (L 160)

Sister Honorine saw the remark as a prophecy. The fact is that Bernadette did begin to have remissions in her asthma crises.

The Franco-Prussian War (1870) did not trouble her. When the Prussians approached Nevers in the autumn of 1870, Bernadette simply said:

'I fear only bad Catholics' (L 174).

On November of that year she wrote:

> They say that the enemy is approaching Nevers. I could do without seeing the Prussians, but I am not afraid of them. God is everywhere, even among the Prussians ... When I was very young, I heard people talking after Reverend Father had given a sermon. They were saying: 'Bah! He's just minding his own business.'
> 'I think that the Prussians are also minding their business' (CROS 3, p. 223, ESB, p. 279).

## The death of Bernadette's father

That letter was the last her father received from her. A short time later, Sister Madeleine Bounaix found her leaning against the chimney in tears. She had just received the news that her father, François Soubirous, had died on March 4, 1871. The date, March 4, was the anniversary of the last apparition in the fifteen-days series. François had been quick to travel to see Bernadette when she was not at home in Lourdes. But he never left his native Pyrenees and he never came to see her in Nevers. Bernadette did not hide her grief when she wrote to her sister, Marie, on March 9:

My tears are joined with yours now. But let us always remain subject, however greatly afflicted, to the paternal hand that is striking us so hard lately. Let us bear and embrace the cross (ESB, p. 282).

It is in the same spirit that she accepted the war as a sign of the time.

## A tribute to her intelligence

On September 3, 1872, she received a high tribute from Doctor Robert Saint-Cyr, the physician of the motherhouse who was also the president of the Nièvre Medical Association:

An infirmarian who fulfils her task to perfection. Small and puny, she is 27 years old. She has a calm and gentle nature. She takes care of her sick patients with a great deal of intelligence, leaving out nothing in the prescriptions ordered. She also exercises great authority and has my full confidence (ESB p. 309).

These lines were written in response to questions raised

by a public statement made by Doctor Voisin, who
worked in the Salpêtrière asylum for aged and mentally ill
women in Paris. Doctor Voisin maintained that:

> The miracle of Lourdes had been sanctioned on the
> testimony of a child suffering from hallucinations who is
> now shut away in the convent of the Ursulines of Nev-
> ers (ESB, p. 309).

### Her peak period (May 1870–1872)

Bernadette had her best period from May 15, 1870 to the
beginning of 1872. She could write about her health without any reservations:

> My health is quite good (December 25, 1870; ESB, p.
> 280).
> My health is terrific (1872; ESB, p. 316).

There were a couple of asthma attacks, but in January
1872 she could paint this reassuring picture:

> My health is only a little worse than last year. It is only
> the severe cold of this winter that gives me some
> difficulty. I have a little more difficulty in breathing.

### A relapse

She suffered a relapse the following winter (1872–1873).
She was put in the 'Sainte-Julienne' wing of the infirmary
on January 17, 1873 (*Journal de la communauté*). On
February 3, she was still 'very ill' (ibid: see L 318). There
was another relapse at Easter (April 13). She must 'stay in
bed' for fifteen days (ESB, p. 321; see page 319).

On May 12, 1873, Mother Joséphine Imbert, the

Superior General, was able to take her in a carriage to the Varennes orphanage. The visit of the two women was a big festive occasion. But Bernadette was treated as a convalescent and seated in a wheel-chair. It was in that chair that she uttered her exhortation to the orphans:

'My children, have real love for the holy Virgin ... Pray to her conscientiously. She will protect you' (L 320).

On June 3, the relapse was more serious. It was at least the third time that she received the Anointing of the Sick (*Journal de la Communauté*). Soon afterwards, however, she resumed her tasks. To those who were happy to see her up and around again she said:

They didn't want me at all up there (L 325).

However, she was discharged from her job on October 30, 1873.

## A spiritual and psychotherapeutic resource

The step was not taken without regrets. Her position as infirmarian afforded an opportunity to send novices with problems to her, either to get care from her or simply to live in her presence. Bernadette's advice, simplicity, and stimulating vigour worked wonders. She was a spiritual and psychotherapeutic resource in the mother-house. Even though she was a professed nun, Mother Marie-Thérèse would often invite her to participate in the recreation of the novices (B 2, p. 122).

One of her frustrations was that they would send her packing when Henri Lasserre's *Histoire des apparitions* was being read to the community. But what could they do. Hadn't the author made the Sisters promise that 'Bernadette would never read this book' (B 2, 126–128)?

Bernadette was not fooled by the brusque dismissals. One day Julie Garros asked her why she was being dismissed so soon.

'Because they want to read something about Lourdes, they show me the door' (L 233).

On the other hand Bernadette was invited to recount the story of apparitions again on June 1, 1869, to four new arrivals. Again the point was made that no one was to speak to her about it further after that. Sometimes the exception does confirm the rule.

The community could make such free use of Bernadette because she herself was so strict about staying in her place and discouraging all signs of veneration or exaltation. One day the novices were just a bit too ostentatious in welcoming her after she had been absent for a long time. Bernadette was angry.

'Because you do me honour that I do not deserve, I will not stay with you during recreation.'

Sister Clémence Chasan tells what happened next:

It was only with great difficulty that we managed to get her to stay. We had to promise to be more simple with her. Then she edified us all with her simplicity and her gaiety (L 272).

Her tonic laughter discouraged all affectation, as Sister Éléonore Bonnet learned at her own expense. To show off her beautiful voice, she sang a little song for the novices with just a few too many fanciful touches. Bernadette's laughter was not appreciated.

'You intimidated me,' protested Sister Éléonore.

'It's true that I did laugh,' replied Bernadette, 'but you will admit that there was a point to it' (L 265).

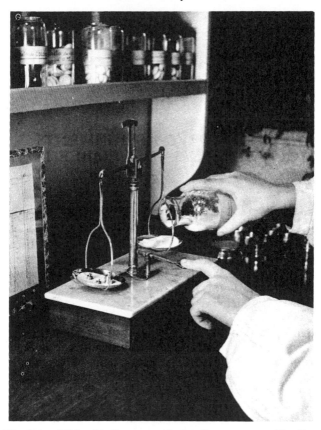

*The Saint-Gildard infirmary with the dispensary used by Bernadette*

# 12

# LAST ACTIVE ASSIGNMENTS
# (OCTOBER 1873—DECEMBER 1874)

On November 5, 1873, Sister Gabriel de Vigouroux, aged 27, was named infirmarian. Bernadette, now 29, became simply the assistant-infirmarian once again. She had never officially held the chief job, though she had done the work. It was not easy for her to change roles; she had the infirmary well in hand. It was hard to move down from the top job with its responsibilities to a subordinate role. When Bernadette offered good reasons for her viewpoint and way of doing things, the new chief infirmarian accused her of pride (L 683). This may help to explain Bernadette's resolution at the end of her retreat in July 1875: i.e., to strive to become *indifferent*.

**Lessons for Julie**

In January 1874, she served as assistant-sacristan as well as assistant-infirmarian. She dressed the choir-boys and she washed and ironed the purificators that had already been cleansed in three successive washings by the priest himself.

She also handled painful jobs in the infirmary. Julie Garros, her former companion and tutor in Lourdes, had entered the convent in Nevers. She was sent to the infirmary to be trained in caring for the sick. She recounts the following incident:

One day Bernadette ordered me to take a walk with Mother Anne-Marie Lescure, who was blind.

'You will take care of her as if it were the good God himself,' said Bernadette.

'Oh, there's a big difference,' I replied.

I asked her why the patient did not have on her full religious habit.

'You will come and see this evening,' said Bernadette.

So I went and saw the sore of the sick nun, crawling with worms that Bernadette was siphoning off onto a dish. I could not stand the sight.

'What a Sister of Charity you will make! You haven't much faith,' Bernadette said to me.

The next morning I returned and helped to dress the sick woman, but without touching the sore. Bernadette did the dressing very tenderly.

When the nun died on June 29, 1874, Bernadette invited Julie to help prepare her for burial.

'I didn't want to, out of aversion.'

'You are a coward,' said Bernadette. 'You will never make a Sister of Charity.'

When the dead woman was dressed, the Sisters came to embrace her. It cost me a great deal to follow their example. I did it, but it sickened me.

'A Sister of Charity who cannot touch the dead! Who ever heard of that?' said Bernadette (L 350).

Bernadette knew the kind of person she was dealing with. Julie had a lively sensitivity but a temperament of iron. Provocation and stimulation were good for her. During the canonization process she displayed great verve and joy in recounting that memory and other ones relating to Bernadette.

It was Bernadette herself who put Julie's head-piece on her the day she took her habit.

'All the ones I put on are solid,' she said (L 289).

Julie remembered the words of advice that Bernadette gave her on July 14, 1874, when she went out to work as an infirmarian. Wordly wise from her experience helping in a hostelry, Bernadette told her:

'When you are in a room with men, make sure that the door is always open' (L 351).

She placed great emphasis on caring for the sick:

'Always remember to see our Lord in the person of the poor ... The more disgusting the poor person is, the more one must love him or her' (L 356).

'When you are taking care of a sick person ... you must withdraw before getting any thanks ... The honour of caring for them is sufficient recompense for us' (L 357).

It was on that note that the two friends parted never to see each other again. Bernadette told her:

'There is no need to give each other souvenirs when we truly love each other ... We must love without measure and dedicate ourselves to our work without counting the cost ... Let us embrace now for the last time' (L 360).

'Accept sickness as a caress,' Bernadette added. 'Spend your all in the service of the poor, but prudently. Never let yourself give way to discouragement. Have real love for the holy Virgin.'

### Bernadette's indifference to affronts

Sister Victorine Poux visited Bernadette in September 1874. She reminded Bernadette how the latter used to flare up like a savage back in the Lourdes hospice, particularly in reaction to 'little injustices' and 'false accusations'.

'Now I am indifferent,' replied Bernadette (L 368).

It was true. She proved it a short time later when Mother Joséphine treated her and Sister Casimir as 'useless people'. Sister Casimir gave way to tears.

'Is that all that's bothering you?' remarked Bernadette. 'Please be good enough to cut it out! You'll see a lot more of it' (L 435; B 2, p. 180).

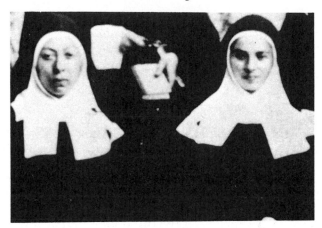

*Bernadette and Sister Victorine Poux*

Bernadette moved towards a serenity grounded in obedience; it had long eluded her and caused her much difficulty to achieve.

The confrontations with the new infirmarian, Sister Gabriel, were painful for Bernadette; but there was no rancour. In fact she made an exception for Sister Gabriel in October 1874. She recounted the facts of the apparitions to her. Bernadette ended her account with the same words she had used to finish her written account of August 22, 1864: 'She had blue eyes' (H 1, p. 61, line 500).

# 13

# IN THE SERVICE OF SICKNESS
## (1875–1878)

From 1875 on the story of Bernadette's life in inextricably bound up with that of her illnesses. Henceforth 'useless', she made every effort to shoulder her new situation as a 'job' in the service of God. 'The job of sickness', she herself would call it.

### Helping others

It was a fruitful task because it was a good opportunity to send novices to help out in the infirmary. There they could profit from the witness of Bernadette, who always remained more attentive to others than to herself. She was a living sermon in her simplicity. As soon as her health improved, she found ingenious ways to help out. She marked the pages in the books being read for the other patients (Sister Joséphine). She taught Sister Rosalie, a novice, how to fold a veil. And her diagnoses remained keen. In 1873, when Julie Garros was discouraged and wanted to leave—as this fiery and impatient girl often felt like doing—Bernadette chatted jokingly with her to get her back on the track. But she was not so successful with Marie Champagnan, who entered the mother-house on August 31, 1875, at the age of 19.

'She still needs her mother,' said Bernadette to Sister Ursule Millien (L 378).

Events seemed to prove that Bernadette was right. On September 14, the postulant left and went back home.

When Sister Joseph Cassagnes was down-spirited with homesickness, Bernadette adopted the language of Jean Vianney, the Curé of Ars, to buck up her spirits.

'Don't you see that it's just the old devil ... When he comes near you, you must spit in his eye' (L 416).

To Sister Casimir Callery, whose father died suddenly in upsetting circumstances, Bernadette said:

> Don't be distraught ... The good God would not permit the parents of nuns to be damned. He gives them a special grace for the sacrifice they have made. ... My mother died on December 8, 1866. The holy Virgin wants me to realize that I should love only her and trust only in her ... that she is to replace my mother ... (L 433).

### Return to Lourdes?

At the end of June 1876, a whole delegation from Nevers was on its way to Lourdes for the consecration of the basilica and the coronation of the statue. The travellers came to see Bernadette and to get her messages and letters. She commended her family to Father Perreau, making special reference to her little brother, Pierre-Bernard:

> For them she did not want so much health and an easy life as virtue and the practice of their religious obligations. ... She regarded certain trials they had been subjected to as chastisements because, so she said, God could not bless those things (L 441).

Before leaving, the new bishop of Nevers, Ladoue, asked her whether she would like to go to Lourdes.

'Oh no, Your Excellency,' she replied. 'I prefer to be in my bed' (L 400).

To others she offered a dreamy reply:

> If I could transport myself in a balloon to the grotto and pray there for a few moments when no one was there, then I would gladly go. But if it is a question of travelling like everyone else and being in a crowd of people, then I prefer to stay here (Reply to Sister Ambroise Fenasse, Superior of the main hospital of Saint-Étienne; L 402).

On other occasions she made similar remarks:

> If I could see it without being seen (L 399).

> I have sacrificed Lourdes. I will see the holy Virgin in heaven. That will be more beautiful (L 401).

Photos of the re-constructed grotto cause her to exclaim: 'Oh my poor grotto! I would not recognize it any more' (L 390).

It was a 'sacrifice' for her even to talk about it. One of her visitors did not insist on pursuing the topic:

> 'I got the impression that we were causing her pain by dwelling on the matter.... We took our leave of her' (L 454).

Bernadette gave private messages for her parish priest, Dean Peyramale. He was greatly upset by the fact that he had been ousted from control of the pilgrimage that he himself founded. Now he found himself without resources, faced with an empty parish church. When he got Bernadette's messages, he had a response sent to her:

> Tell her that she is still my child and that I give her my blessing (L 398).

The following year Bernadette learnt of his death. It occurred on Saturday, September 8, 1877, the feast of the

Birth of Our Lady. The news was brought by messenger to the convent. Sister Nathalie Portat conveyed it to Bernadette, who was praying in the church loft. Bernadette shed tears for Dean Peyramale too.

## Health report (1875–1877)

During these years Bernadette's illness continued, with the disturbing ups and downs that typify her condition. It was the very substance of her existence.

In 1875 she kept to her bed from April to mid-June (GUYNOT, 1936, p. 201), was back on her feet during the summer, and suffered a relapse in October (*Journal de la communauté*). On November 19, an attack of blood-spitting raised fears for her life. She remained in bed until May 1876. The fine weather gave her new life. In June she attended Mass on Sunday, something which she had missed for six months (ESB, p. 475). But she could only get there by 'being carried' (Letter of June 27, 1876; ESB, p. 428).

Her stomach seemed averse to nourishment. She was 'always broken-down' she admitted, in her letter of June 25, 1876 to Mother Alexandrine Roques. Such an admission was unusual for her because she tended to talk only about the bright side of things and her optimism vis-a-vis the future (ESB, p. 424). She employed her strength as much as she could. In August 1876, for example, Sister Joseph Biermann found her sweeping the infirmary. She took away Bernadette's broom, but the latter grabbed it back.

'You shan't have it. Conquer or die' (L 413), said Bernadette jokingly.

Here we see the martial side of Bernadette's spirit, stirred by the military deeds of her godfather who won so much honour in the battle of Solferino. A book she was reading in the same summer of 1876 (title unknown) prompted her to make this comment:

'Oh, this book makes me want to go off to war!' (L 417).

Her letters of August and September assured people that she was 'suffering very little' or 'not too much' (ESB, p. 434–436). But she could not hide the fact that she was suffering from 'a weakness that nothing comes close to'. She had to cut short her letter of September 7:

'My hand is trembling like that of an old woman' (ESB 437).

The same thing happened on September 13, when she was writing to Rachel Dufo:

'I leave you here. I cannot hold my pen. I hardly know what I am saying to you. Adieu!' (ESB, p. 439).

Writing to Rachel, an upper-middle class girl from Lourdes who became a friend after the apparitions, Bernadette switched between the formal *vous* and the informal *tu*.

Her November letters assured people that she was better (ESB, pp. 444–447). *But it was always when she was feeling better that she wrote to people*. Here was the paradoxical side of her correspondence: although her health was basically going downhill, she informed people in an ordinary way of her improvement. And she stressed the good care that was being given to her, as if she were 'a little baby' (ESB, p. 434).

### A letter to the Pope

On December 16, 1876, she was visited by the new bishop of Nevers, Bishop de Ladoue. Forcade had been made Archbishop of Aix in 1873.

'He is small and cold. He will not last long', said Bernadette after an earlier visit (L 338). In fact Bishop de Ladoue was to die on July 23, 1877.

This time he had come to the infirmary because he intended to carry a letter written by Bernadette herself to Pope Pius IX. She wrote it in bed, using a little wooden desk that was placed on her knees. One of her knees was painful.

Her first draft was examined and revised as if it were a conciliar text. After all, this letter was for the Pope himself. In it Bernadette had naïvely reiterated the remark that the bishop had made to convince her to write the letter: 'The best way to get a blessing is to write a letter.' One simply could not expose the tactics of a bishop like that!

Moreover, Bernadette was too free and easy in her style. It was a point in time when the papal Zouaves (recruited mostly from France) stood out as symbols of loyalty and devotion to the Pope. Bernadette had written:

> For a long time now I have been a Zouave, however unworthy, of Your Holiness. My weapons are prayer and sacrifice.

The idea was good and should be retained. It might well touch the heart of the Holy Father. But a little bit more modesty and formality was in order, like this:

> For some years now I have constituted myself, unworthy though I be, as a little Zouave of your Holiness.

In her first draft Bernadette finished as follows:

> From heaven the most holy Virgin must often cast her gaze on You, most Holy Father, since You proclaimed her to be the Immaculate one and then, four years later, this good Mother came to earth to say: 'I am the Immaculate.'

> I did not know what that meant. I had not even heard the word. Later, after thinking it over, I say to myself: 'The holy Virgin is nice. One could say that she came to confirm the word of our Holy Father.'

Well, that ending was just a little too abrupt. It would have to be stretched out a bit by adding a few more solemn phrases and qualifying adjectives. (That was hardly Bernadette's style, of course.) So the revised ending of the letter reads:

I hope that ... this good Mother ... will deign once again to put her foot on the head of the accursed serpent and thus put an end to the cruel trials of the holy Church and to the sufferings of her august and well beloved Pontiff.

A nun re-copied the second draft on the official monogrammed stationery of the congregation (ESB, p. 458). Then Bernadette wrote out the letter again in her best handwriting, the little wooden desk still perched on her sore knee. She got rather confused when she came to the queer ending and jumbled it up a bit (ESB, p. 451). And there were also spelling mistakes! That letter couldn't possibly be sent to the Pope! She must write it again, despite her sore knee and her weariness. Somehow she managed to do it again, and this final copy was conveyed to Pius IX by Bishop de Ladoue (ESB, pp. 448–456). On January 14, 1877, he brought the promised blessing back from Rome.

The year 1876 ended badly for Bernadette, even though she wrote as follows to Father Pomian on December 28:

My stomach ... not very obliging ... has been keeping down a little more food for about a month (ESB, p. 473).

Yet the fact was that she had scarcely left her bed during the whole year, as she wrote to Dean Peyramale that same day:

Well, it is now a whole year that I am in my white chapel (ESB, p. 475).

She had only been out of bed for brief periods during the summer. And she left the infirmary only to go to Mass, with others taking her there by one means or another.

## A marked recovery (Summer 1877)

A surprising improvement took place during the summer of 1877. In a letter to Pierre Soubirous dated July 17, 1877, she wrote:

> I take a walk in the garden every day to restore my strength (ESB, p. 486).

To Father Pomian she wrote the following on September 15:

> My health has improved considerably. I can follow a great part of the community's exercises. I take walks and have a good appetite (ESB, p. 491).

She participated in the recreation-periods once again and went around to the different groups, who loved to welcome her. During this period she walked well enough to be given little messenger assignments around the house. In September, assisted by her courage, she managed to climb to the second floor to see Jeanne Jardet, the kitchen maid. The latter was ill and very much wanted to see Bernadette.

That same month she waited a long time in the queue for Confession and 'kept the place' of another Sister: Irène Ganier. In October her good health held up, so much so that her companions lifted her up (she was so light) to pick a grape high up on the wall, overlooked during the harvest (RC, p. 84–85; L 477).

On the feast of the Presentation (November 21, 1877), she came downstairs again for the renewal of vows. And it was she who read the pledge of renewal in the name of the participants.

**Winter 1877–1878**

In December 1877, Bernadette was again confined to her room. Her knee was the problem. But she did manage to get up to help the novices with the Christmas crib. It was she who placed the infant Jesus in the crib:

'You must have been quite cold, my poor little Jesus, in the stable of Bethlehem. . . . How heartless the inhabitants of Bethlehem must have been not to show hospitality to the infant Jesus' (L 484).

But ill health took over. Sister Ambroise Fenasse came to Nevers for the chapter meeting of January 28, 1878, at which Mother Adélaïde Dons was elected Superior General. She found 'Sister Marie-Bernard immobilized on her bed by a white tumour on her knee with a silicate dressing' (L 499).

The silicate was an advanced treatment for that day, according to Doctor Flament, but of course it is outmoded today.

On February 10, Bernadette suffered a relapse and spat blood (*Journal de la Communauté*). Again she had to be watched over during the night. Her own concern, as always, was that her attendants get some sleep.

'Don't trouble yourself so often,' she said to Sister Julie Durand. 'They think I am going to die. But I still have more than six months to go' (L 501).

Her asthma choked her often and she needed air. But contemporary custom advised people 'never to go to bed with the windows open because it is too easy to catch cold or to contract rheumatic pains'. Bernadette was not easily put off. It was customary to open the window upon waking up in the morning, so she asked Julie Durand to do this 'at 5:30 a.m.' It was May of the year 1878, but even then Bernadette did not get away with it. Mother Vauzou passed by one morning and saw the open window.

'Foolhardy creature that you are! Why have you opened the casement window? To make your cold even worse?'

Sister Julie Durand hastened to close the window as Mother Vauzou departed. Bernadette stopped her with a gesture.

'Wait! Our Mother did not say to close it. She simply scolded me for having had it opened' (L 505).

Thus we see that Bernadette remained a free creature. Her keen peasant casuistry, which we saw her use earlier with Julie Garros in the case of the strawberries, had not been forgotten.

## The last summer

In September 1878 she was suffering a great deal from the worsening sore on her knee. However, she was able to go to the chapel to hear the words of the preacher who was preparing the community for the profession of perpetual vows. Somehow or other she even managed to kneel down during the exercises. But she had to give the whole thing up before the preparatory days were over.

'I can't handle it any more. I won't come back again. I will remain in the infirmary,' she said, towards the end of the retreat (L 517).

She did come down to the chapel on September 22 for the renewal of vows, reading the formula established in the new constitutions of 1870:

I, Sister Marie-Bernard, wishing to consecrate myself to the service of God and charitable works in the congregation of the Sisters of Charity and Christian Instruction established in the diocese of Nevers, do hereby vow myself for the rest of my life to poverty, chastity, and obedience in the manner expressed in the constitutions of this congregation. I pray that Our Lord Jesus Christ, through the intercession of the holy Virgin, my good Mother, will give me the grace to fulfil these commitments faithfully.

After the ceremony she congratulated the singers for their fine work:

'I thought I was in heaven,' she said twice that day. 'If I were dead, I would be sure of my fate because the profession of vows is a second Baptism' (L 519–520).

'Look for nothing better on earth' (L 529).

## Her white chapel

On October 30, 1878, the infirmary for professed nuns was opened on the first floor, in the Sainte Croix room. It was in the other wing of the mother-house. Bernadette moved into her final dwelling place on earth.

On November 12 and November 13 she was able to come to the ground floor to meet the new postulants. She noticed that one of them was down in the dumps.

'Are you feeling bad?'

'Oh yes, very bad!'

'Don't worry, you'll persevere in the congregation,' said Bernadette, putting her arm around her shoulder (L 530).

On December 11, 1878, she took up permanent residence in her 'white chapel', as she called her big curtained bed. She had set up an image of St Bernard alongside the bed.

'You pray to your patron, I see,' said Sister Agatha.

'Oh yes, I pray to him well enough, but I don't imitate him at all. Saint Bernard loved suffering. I avoid it as much as I can' (L 410).

In an age when people talked a great deal, and rather wrongheadedly, about 'loving suffering', Bernadette herself never succeeded in becoming a masochist.

Bernadette felt herself slipping into a new or second childhood. Her vigour, her memory, and her vivacity were weakening. She went back to fashioning the little altars and religious decorations that she loved to make in the

Gaol and in the fields of Bartrès. One picture symbolized the Masses being said around the clock all over the world.

'I unite myself with all these Masses, especially during the night when I sometimes get no sleep,' she said to Sister Ambroise Fenasse in January 1879.

But she did not want to end with a sad reminder of her sleepless nights.

'The thing that bothers me is this little choir-boy who never rings the bell ... I sometimes feel like giving him a good shaking' (L 500).

Immobilized, Bernadette used her remaining reserves of strength as best she could. In August 1876, Sister Agathe had found her 'sitting up in bed, shredding linen for rags'. From Easter 1877 on, she spent a great deal of time painting or embroidering hearts. In accordance with the devotional practice of the epoch, she distributed them to different people with a gay remark.

No one can say that Sister Marie-Bernard has no heart (L 462).

If people tell you that I have no heart, tell them that I make them all day long (L 463).

In October 1878, Sister Thérèse Lacoste found her colouring little images and 'sketching the crown of thorns around the Sacred Heart'. With a mixture of mischievousness and seriousness she told Sister Thérèse:

If you want to be a nun, Mademoiselle, you must learn to love suffering. Our Lord gives his crown of thorns to his friends (L 529).

## Good for nothing

It was not suffering but inactivity that bothered her most.

'Always in the infirmary, always "good for nothing",' she said, reiterating the expression that came up in her first conversation with the bishop about her vocation and which had been emphasized when she received her first official assignment.

She added: 'The good God has seen fit not to let me choose my own type of life. I certainly would not have chosen the state of inactivity to which I am reduced. I would really have liked to be actively employed at something!'

'You pray for those who do not pray,' said Sister Victoire Cassou to her.

'That is all I have to do. . . . My prayer is my only weapon. I can only pray and suffer' (L 515).

She had already voiced that theme in her letter to Pope Pius IX:

> My weapons are prayer and sacrifice, and I will keep them until my last breath. Then, finally, the weapon of suffering will fall from my hand. But the weapon of prayer will follow me to heaven, where it will be even more powerful (ESB, p. 453).

### Overcome by joy

A breath of merciful grace entered Saint Gildard with the arrival of Father Febvre in September 1875. 43 years old, he replaced Father Douce as the chaplain in the mother-house. Bernadette had symbolized the austerity of Father Douce in a little acrostic:

D ouleur (suffering)
O ubli (forgetfulness)
U nion (union)
C onfiance (trust)
E prouvant (trying)

Bernadette softened the last item by replacing the word

*The white chapel*

*eprouvant* with the word *exigeant* ('demanding'). By now
there was Father Febvre, who was encouraging and help-
ful, just as Bernadette tried to be to others. Tact, penetra-
tion, and docility in the face of the will of God were the
charisms of his ministry.

In October 1877, one of his sermons brought great joy
to Bernadette. Sister Casimir Callery reported the conversation:

'Oh, Seraph, how content I am!'
Sister Marie-Bernard called me 'Seraph' because in the
dialogue recited for the feast of our Mother Mistress, I
was the Seraph. The name Casimir did not come to her
because she had never heard it until I came along. . . .
'What's up with you, then?'
'Didn't you hear the sermon?'
'Yes, of course.'
'Well, the chaplain said that when one does not want to
sin, one does not.'
'Yes, I heard that. So?'
'So I have never willed to commit a sin. That means I
have not!'
Joy lit up her face . . . I envied her happiness because I
could not say as much (L 420).

# 14

# THE DAY-TO-DAY HOLINESS OF BERNADETTE

We have almost come to the end of Bernadette's life. She was soon to undergo that mysterious passage to the hereafter, a trip that every human being makes with a certain degree of solitude. We can only view it 'from behind', as one doctor who has studied the phenomenon of death and dying has pointed out.

Bernadette accomplished this passage amid a series of mysterious trials and a dark night of the soul. She was not only afflicted with physical suffering. She also suffered from a dark night of faith and hope as well, as we shall see more fully in Chapter 16.

After the transparent light of the apparitions, Bernadette returned to the normal state of faith in her daily life. But it was a sky lit up with stars, as it were. Now she entered a dark night without any stars at all. The final obscurity of Bernadette and her destiny links up with the initial obscurity of her early childhood; but it stands on a new level of silence, secretness, and poverty. For those who approached her, however, it was a night embodying the radiance of God. Perhaps it will also be that for us, as we follow her in the final stage of her life.

At the start of this book we discerned the invigorating and surprising light of the Gospel message in the passion and suffering of her childhood poverty and her disdained social status. The final passion of her passage to the hereafter is even more luminous in that sense, but it is also even more secret.

## Her interior axis

If we seek to glimpse the divine radiance in the daily words and actions of Bernadette which have been described in these pages, then we must grasp the axis of her life. Hers was a day-to-day holiness devoid of super-structures, ideology, lengthy discourses, and any trace of complacency. Her holiness flowed from a basic inner orientation that gave unity to her life. We can lay hold of the starting points and end point of that orientation, even though her inner life is hidden in shadows and mist. For she followed the same basic line throughout her life: in sickness and in health, in the open air and the cloister, in moments of glory and moments of humiliation.

Her inner axis was glimpsed clearly by Father Febvre, her last confessor. The keenest of all, he was the best at recognizing and respecting her particular grace. This is what he wrote:

> When the humble Bernadette knocked at the door of the convent of the Sisters of Nevers ... she already possessed certain lights, certain teachings, and a line of conduct that would give her direction and also help her spiritual directors and superiors to guide her on the pathways to perfection. Meditating on the words, recommendations, and secrets communicated to her by the Immaculate Conception and acquiring a deeper understanding of the mysterious actions she performed in the grotto, Bernadette was to formulate rules of conduct that would enable her to arrive at the ideal of sanctity asked of her.
>
> Moreover, like the prophets of the old law whose lives and actions were a visible confirmation of the great truths they proclaimed, Bernadette's mission would not

just be to transmit the wishes of heaven. She would also practice works that gave expression to this message. Her habitual state of suffering would reveal to souls the pathway and the necessity of suffering for those who wished to be 'happy not in this world but the next'.

In her heart Bernadette was to feel the same force that pushed her towards the grotto in Lourdes to receive the visits of our Lady. And these mysterious impulses would be no less potent in driving her to practice.

The words of Father Febvre are a bit lustreless. His language, like Bernadette's own life, is wrapped up in the narrow pigeon-holes of the nineteenth century. We must strip off the outer crust to get to the illuminating centre within. The wondrous Christian generosity of people in those days was exercised within the framework of cultural poverty and heavy juridical bonds. In the nineteenth century the congregation of the Sisters of Nevers, founded under the evangelical inspiration of Dom de Laveyne (1683), was submerged under the waters of canonical legalism and a straitened concept of obedience. Thus, during Bernadette's own lifetime, the order's fourth vow of charity was suppressed by Rome because it could not be reduced to canonical forms. Caught in the narrow confines of this whole framework, Bernadette still managed to grasp and hold on to the essential message of the Gospel and to link up with the basic inspiration of Dom de Laveyne. That is the basic fact which Father Febvre managed to see, in his own way.

Father Febvre came to realize that the axis of Bernadette's holiness was an *inner* one prompted by the Holy Spirit. It was something imposed on Bernadette herself, and hence on those who had the task of giving her direction.

This inner axis was not just the corpus of words that she heard from the apparitions. Her life and actions welled up from a basic impulse rooted within. She did not practice the message of Lourdes as one might implement a rule or a law. The inner spring of all her prophetic or mystical actions was love, and it was through love that she fulfilled the law. She did not rely on tiresome discourses or ready-made formulas.

This inner dynamism was hers prior to the apparitions. Long before, she had learned to grasp the Gospel message at its very source. The apparitions at Massabielle were to intensify and channel this impulse, and her religious life, even more, would help her to shoulder it.

Thus the axis of Bernadette's holiness was the message of Lourdes, but the latter was rooted in that prior, inner source which gave rise to Bernadette's actions as they expressed it.

**Embodying the message of Lourdes**

The message of Lourdes is not restricted to the words Bernadette heard in the grotto: i.e., *prayer* and *penitence*, in the Gospel sense of thoroughgoing *conversion* or *turning towards God*. It is to be found, first and foremost, in the *poverty* embodied in the very choice of Bernadette and in the immediate response of the poor to the good news. Jacomet, the police commissioner, bears unmistakable witness to this fact. Finally, the message of Lourdes is ultimately the very name and identity of the messenger, the *immaculate* Mary, the Virgin of the *Magnificat*, the prototype of the Church and of a radical and total living out of the gospel.

Here the apparition reveals its full meaning. Bernadette received a great deal from that encounter with the mother of Christ in the communion of saints that became transparent for a brief moment. The meeting took place in a concrete, visible form that Bernadette could understand on the basis of the tradition that had come down to her. The Virgin appeared to her as a living icon. Contemplating this woman, who was preceded and enveloped in a light 'like that of the sun breaking through the darkness',

Bernadette gained a better understanding of what she was already living amid the obscurity of faith. The various attitudes and poses of the apparition—her prayer, her smiles, her sad glances—reflected her compassion for sinners. The surrounding crowd saw all these reflected on the face of Bernadette in her transparent ecstasy: head erect, her face looking upward. Bernadette simply modelled herself after the Virgin Mary: the chief handiwork of God, the shaper of Jesus' humanity, and the prototype of the Church.

When I finished the work of examining and collating the chance words of Bernadette, I was greatly surprised to see that they almost grouped themselves under the key words of the message of Lourdes: *poverty*, *prayer*, and *penance*. These are the lines of force that inspired Bernadette's life. Her deeds blossomed from this interior sap as the leaves of a tree blossom from within. Bernadette, modest flower that she was, resembled the model that she had always sensed near her and that appeared to her in the grotto: *Mary Immaculate*, the messenger of the Bible of the poor.

## God is love

Once one has grouped the words of Bernadette around the four themes mentioned above (poverty, prayer, penance, and Mary Immaculate), there remains a final set of words that are also important, indeed essential. They relate to two other key words situated on the same axis. One is *charity* in the fullest sense of the word (Greek *agapē*): the unique love shared and communicated which is the whole of the Trinity and of the Church. The other word is *God*, or 'God alone' (L 857), as Bernadette once put it.

The two latter words reflect the spirituality of Dom de Laveyne, the founder of the Sister of Charity of Nevers. The first term, *charity*, is inscribed over the doorway of Saint Gildard: *Dieu est Charité*. And the formula *Dieu seul*

('God alone') is on the blazon of the congregation.

However, Dom de Laveyne took these words from the Gospel message, of which they are the very essence. As far back as we know her, Bernadette was in full agreement on this essential point. She always went back to the same source. She knew how to scrape away the surrounding mire to get at the core, even as she managed to dig out the spring at the grotto.

The basic elements of the message of Lourdes—prayer, poverty, and penitence—are the prolegomena to the Gospels. They are inscribed in Mary's *Magnificat*, in the preaching of John the Baptist, and in the message of the Beatitudes. The other two expressions which sum up the inner and outer life of Bernadette—charity and God alone—are the very essence and epitome of the Gospels. Thanks to the inner working of the Holy Spirit, Bernadette brought all these values together almost by instinct.

Thus we find a pre-established harmony between Bernadette's own spirituality and that of the congregation in which she lived her life. For according to Father Ravier, the major themes which serve as an inspiration for that congregation are prayer, penitence, poverty, service to souls, and charity towards the sick and the poor (ESB, p. 228). They are the axes of Bernadette's religious life too. Anyone will be able to recognize them in her life and her deeds, and they need hardly be spelled out here.

But we must go back one step further. These evangelical axes are evident as far back as Bernadette's childhood prior to the apparitions. They simply show that her life was almost like a straight line drawn from a single point. Her spiritual line was grounded on the robust simplicity of her nature and the basic bedrocks that gave her security from infancy onwards. The love which pervaded her family life remained a profound source of strength to her always. The trials which afflicted Bernadette from the age of ten, her struggles as a little servant-girl in Bartrès, and the poverty and disdain to which she was subjected only helped to highlight a gift that was hers always. She had received it from a living Christian tradition framed in the trappings of a certain time and place, and with a sure spiritual instinct she made it her own. Her instinct was rooted in her Baptism, and it flowed from there as water from a spring.

*Bernadette's sheepfold in Bartrès*

# 15

# THE TRIALS OF BERNADETTE

We are now almost ready to follow Bernadette through the last months of her life. But before we do that (in Chapters 17 and 18), and before we consider the phases of her last dark night of the soul (in Chapter 16), we must pause for a moment to consider the crescendo of little trials that Bernadette faced every day in her life as a nun, right up until the end.

It is an important matter because it relates to one of the first messages she received from the apparition. And it was the most paradoxical and troubling message of all:

I do not promise to make you happy in this world, but in the next (Message of February 18, 1858).

This eschatological promise oriented Bernadette towards the ultimate realities and severed her from all human supports in this world. It was an abrupt promise evoking the *via negativa*, the dark night of the soul and the nothingness of which St John of the Cross spoke.

So let us consider the little trials that formed the tissue of Bernadette's everyday life as a nun and prepared her for the final testing.

## Lourdes so far away

The first trial in Bernadette's life as a nun, the one that

drew tears from her the first Sunday she was in the Saint Gildard convent, was the uprooting from her beloved home territory and nostalgia for her Bigorre countryside—for the grotto especially. To be sure, she surmounted this nostalgia and regret, not only with determination but also with humour. Her tears watered her vocation and fashioned a rainbow at the end.

Given the tenacious shrewdness that was hers, and that was quite evident when she decided to leave Bartrès and receive her First Communion, we know that Bernadette the nun could easily have obtained permission to return to Lourdes. At the very least she could have managed this on major occasions. She would have found no lack of supporters, and she knew how to make use of them if she had wanted to. She was very good at coming to the defence of others. But whenever she was asked about returning to Lourdes, her answer was basically the same: no. Here are a sample of her replies to people:

No, never! (to Julie Garros in 1871; L 195).
My place is here (L 405).
I stay in my little corner (L 408).
I have left Lourdes for good (L 510).
To return to Lourdes would be a very great sacrifice for me (L 375).
I am happy to remain here (L 510).
Go back to Lourdes? Oh, I will see Her in heaven (to Sister Ramplou in 1873; L 334).

## Family worries

The second trial, closely linked to the first, was her concern for her family, for she was the eldest child, the 'heir'. Loyal to tradition and to her social relations, Bernadette did not feel that she was now free of those bonds. She suffered over her inability to fulfil these deeply rooted responsibilities. She shared in the joys and sorrows of members of the family. This was particularly true in the case of Toinette, who lost baby after baby. She tried to settle or smooth over family disputes, and she was anxious that her relatives should be faithful to their religious duties (L 406). Distressed that her sister began to engage in selling pious objects in Lourdes, she tried to dissuade her.

'I wrote to her, but she did not pay any attention,' Bernadette confided to Julie Garros, her companion in the Lourdes hospice who had become Sister Vincent (L 198).

Later on, she was to resign herself to the trade of her brother Pierre, but only on the condition that he would adhere to the prevailing precept of 'not selling on Sunday'.

'I don't ask that they be rich, but that they love the good God and be what they ought to be,' she said to Sister Aurélie Gouteyron in October 1873.

The danger of becoming rich through this sort of trade bothered her a great deal. She was willing to accept their involvement in commerce, she told Father Perreau in 1876, who was going to see her relatives:

provided that they do not enrich themselves. Tell them right out not to get rich (L 406).

## Inquisitive visitors

The most irritating trial was undoubtedly the visits, which did not stop when Bernadette got to Nevers even though she thought the matter had been settled (L 662-663). In Lourdes she had faced up to all comers, not without chagrin but in the knowledge that she was the only one who could fulfil that particular task. For only she could tell people what she alone had seen and heard. But once the pilgrimage was established and authorized by the bishop, and once the 'chapel' had been constructed, Bernadette felt that she had turned a corner in her own life. The pilgrimage to Lourdes no longer needed her, and so she had come to Nevers 'to hide herself'.

But that was a difficult, if not impossible, dream. A city set on a mountain cannot be hidden so easily (Mt 5:14). Her superiors were forced to make exceptions to deal with the crowd, and the exceptions were many. The end of retreat-periods was painful for Bernadette because 'people came looking for her as if she were a wild animal in a sideshow' (L 768; her comment to Sister Marie Delbrel).

After her death Father Febvre and her superiors told Father Cros about her 'extreme aversion to parlours'.

You almost had to drag her into one. When you found her—she would go and hide—you had to console her on the way. And she would keep saying: 'Oh how tedious it all is!' (L 760).

Authority would have to be invoked because she, with good reason, would point out her objection: 'You promised me!' Her obedience was not blind. She freely expressed her own proper reactions.

One day one of the Sisters got permission for a relative of hers to see Bernadette. She invited Bernadette to come downstairs, but she was honest enough to tell Bernadette that she was not obliged to do this:

'The Superior permits you to do this, but she leaves it up to you.'

'She leaves it up to me? Then no! No! No!'

And Bernadette headed for the back of the garden (L 763).

Bernadette did not believe in carrying out duties that were no duties at all. In that respect she was free from the masochistic spirit of the time.

When she was performing the duties of sacristan, some people came to observe her during a ceremony of religious profession.

'Sister, where does Bernadette sit?'

'No luck,' she replied, 'today she will not be in her regular place.'

And with that remark she disappeared from the scene.

In February 1871, Sister Victorine Girard arrived at the mother-house. She asked her neighbour in the novitiate if she could show her who Sister Marie-Bernard was. Her neighbour, none other than Bernadette, said that she could. That was all she said. The next day Victorine asked another nun the same question and was surprised to get the following response:

'Why, you were right alongside her yesterday evening' (L 179).

One day Sister Augustin Fort got the Superiors to promenade Bernadette in front of one of the convent towers to 'show' her to a priest who was passing through town. Bernadette caught on to the trick and gestured to the offending nun:

'Oh, my little one, you will pay me for this!' (L 64).

On another occasion Sister Julienne Capmartin was supposed to stop her on her way somewhere so that some people could see her. Sister Julienne improvised a little conversation about the flowers in the area. Bernadette, it seems, got wind of the trap. She kept moving on her way to the linen-room, greeting Sister Julienne with only one remark:

'Blabber-mouth!'

On the other hand Sister Marie-Joseph Berger had more success with the same strategem. But in this case she was not presenting Bernadette to any adult or important person but rather to her little niece, aged three. Bernadette loved children, and she stopped quite willingly. This was a real human relationship, not a peep-show.

One day during a procession a woman picked out Bernadette, placed herself alongside her, and could not hide her somewhat overexcited joy.

'I'm going to play a trick on her', whispered Bernadette to Sister Bernard Dalias. Bernadette slid between the wall and the bench and disappeared into the back of the chapel, much to the woman's dismay.

'You talked too much', said Sister Dalias to the woman (L 450).

Her superiors did all they could to protect Bernadette,

but an exception was made for bishops passing through. They had a right to see her, and the list of those who did is probably far from complete:

> Besides those who occupied the see of Nevers-Forcade, de Ladoue (1873), and Lelong (1877)—the documents permit us to identify some dozen or so prelates. Among them are Bishop Chigi, the Apostolic Nuncio (L 128) and Bishop Dupanloup (L 295).

'Those poor bishops would be better off staying at home in their chanceries', said Bernadette (Testimony of Sister Marie Delbrel; L 766).

When she was told that Bishop Forcade had come with some colleague to see her, Bernadette replied:

'You should say rather that he wishes to have me be seen by someone' (L 765).

To spare Bernadette, efforts were made to show her to people in seemingly accidental circumstances. Sister Victoire Cassou recounts the following incident:

> One day Bishop Bourret of Rodez had come to Saint Gildard and he wanted to see Sister Marie-Bernard. To do that without letting Bernadette know what was up, they decided to use a strategem. The whole community was assembled in the novitiate hall. After he made a few pious remarks, the Superior asked the nuns from the Aveyron province to stand up. Those from the Pyrenees region stood up in their turn. Then the bishop went around so that the nuns might kiss his ring. While he was doing this, the Superior or Mistress of Novices would say something about each one of the Sisters. . . . Well, Sister Marie-Bernard caught on to what this was all about.
>
> 'Relax, I know just what I'm going to do.'
>
> With that remark, she disappeared through a little doorway near her.
>
> So I said to her later: 'What about the 40 days indulgence? (for kissing a bishop's ring).'

'My Jesus mercy! There's 300 days!' she replied.

Bishop Bourret, however, did not give up easily. Indeed he had a revealing conversation with her in which she made a surprising remark about the apparitions (see Chapter 16: 'Dark night all around').

Another bishop, almost certainly Bishop Léseleuc of Kerouara, was admitted to the infirmary to visit a sick Bernadette. He was struck with a more artful idea. Playing negligently with his episcopal cap, he let it drop on her bed. It was a 'deliberate stratagem', designed to get her to pick it up for him. Bernadette did not move a muscle. The conversation dropped to zero also. Finally, the bishop took the initiative:

'Sister, would you mind giving me back my cap?'

'Your Excellency, I did not ask for your cap. You can pick it up yourself', was her reply.

In the end she had to pick it up out of obedience, however, because a superior present in the room ordered her to do so.

### The fight against her savage nature

Bernadette regarded the 'struggle against nature' as one of her most serious and difficult obligations. Readers must remember that this fight against nature was highly prized in those days, and was not without traces of artificiality. In Bernadette's case, fortunately her nature was solid and resourceful. But she regretted that what she regarded as her savagely natural impulses.

'Oh, my impetuous nature again!' she exclaimed on one occasion (L 772).

'Way down in there, we don't see what is going on. We would not earn any merit if we did not master ourselves' (L 773).

She also felt beaten at times: 'I am discouraged' (L 774). But those moments of difficulty rekindled the hope she placed in prayer and the Eucharist. During one crisis, when some thought her last day had arrived, she said:

'Don't worry. I will not die yet. The old human being must die first, and it is still very much alive' (L 775).

Bernadette was flexible in dealing with her problems, however. 'The first impulse is not ours,' she said to Julie Garros, 'but the second one is up to us' (L 253).

She accepted the fact that it would be a long-term battle and prayed accordingly: 'My God, give me patience' (L 558). These trials led her to the cross, her recourse in difficulties.

## A useless servant

Bernadette was hurt a great deal by the fact that she was not able to serve people as she wished to. This was all the more frustrating because it seemed to go against the very purpose of her religious vocation. She did not really mind being treated as a 'useless' person or someone 'good for nothing' (L 499, 523, etc.). What bothered her was *being* useless in fact, being unable to serve others, and being frustrated in her desire to perform the tangible works through which a human being finds self-expression and fulfillment in his or her own eyes and the eyes of others.

## The severity of her superiors

The most celebrated trial, which has inspired authors of books and producers of films, was the severity of her religious superiors towards her: i.e., Mother Joséphine Imbert, the Superior General, who died on May 1, 1878; and especially Mother Marie Thérèse Vauzou, the Mistress of Novices.

The trial was real enough. It was mentioned by many witnesses during the two processes of beatification (L 3, pp. 168–175; and B 2, pp. 244–369). But it has been highly fictionalized and over-exploited to suit the more mythological bent of the popular imagination.

It has been exaggerated on several levels and for various reasons. First of all, the severity of the superiors made a deeper impression on the other nuns when it concerned Bernadette, the seer of Lourdes, who was the object of discreet reverence on their part.

Secondly, the formal canonization process dwelt at length on all the minute details concerned with this matter. For it had a lot to do with such matters as obedience, the heroic practice of virtue, and even the 'objections' against Bernadette's canonization that had to be resolved. If her superiors had treated Bernadette severely, then wasn't it obvious that she deserved such treatment for one reason or another? Excessive concern for all the minor details of convent life is typical in such instances. For example, the canonization process of Thérèse of Lisieux brought to light the quarrels between two rival factions in the Carmelite convent. The situation there was far less normal than it was in the Nevers convent.

Thirdly and finally, some assumed for a long time that behind the acknowledged documents there were other documents buried away. Needless to say, the assumption was that the latter had a much more terrible tale to tell. This myth has been completely exploded by full examination of the materials. I shall not reiterate here what I have examined in great detail in several other works (see L 3, pp. 168–175; and *Bernadette vous parle*, Paris, Lethielleux, II, 344–394).

Here in brief is the whole truth, as far as it can be made out from these investigations. The severity of her superiors is a fact. But it was only a specific instance of a rule applied generally in that austere age. In some convents, far less well balanced than that of Nevers, the mistresses of novices practised a veritable ritual of an initiation that would shock us today. There were no absurdly repugnant or brutal practices at the Saint Gildard convent, but the superiors did try to break the self-will of the novices in order to form them in obedience. The testing was handed out in measured doses, depending on the temperament of the novice in question. In Bernadette's case there was a more specific set of motives involved. Her superiors were concerned not to foster any elitist feelings in her. Her exceptional status presented this danger. And it was not just Bernadette who 'benefited' from a more demanding type of treatment. Her superiors deliberately adopted that approach because they had to guard themselves against a displaced veneration for her.

These reasons seem to account fully for the attitude of Mother Joséphine Imbert, the Superior General. She humiliated Bernadette and treated her coolly for fear that she herself might otherwise treat her with favouritism. One day, on returning from Rome, she spoke a few words to each novice as she embraced her. When she came to Bernadette, she embraced her without saying a word. According to the testimony of Bishop Forcade (page 26), the Superior General treated her as a 'useless person' or even as 'a little fool'.

'Mother Joséphine! Oh, I'm scared of her!' (L 502), said Bernadette.

And that is all we find in the voluminous dossier of confidential remarks spoken under the seal of secrecy.

The case of Mother Marie-Thérèse Vauzou is more complicated. Some of the 'trials' she inflicted on Bernadette were typical: e.g., kissing the ground. It was a commonplace act of penance and humility in those days.

'I would look in vain for a floor-tile in the novitiate that I have not kissed', said Sister Julienne Capmartin (B 2, p. 127). And Bernadette was not the only one to be treated as proud or as a fool.

The overall evaluations of the witnesses differ. 'I would not have liked to have been in her place', said Sister Stéphanie Vareillaud, a fellow-novice, at the beatification process (PANev 327). On the other hand, Sister Julienne Capmartin, who was treated with special severity by Mother Marie-Thérèse, had this to say:

I never noticed anything resembling injustice or real harshness.... She always treated Sister Marie-Bernard like the others—with no special consideration of course, but not unjustly either (GUYNOT, 1926, pp. 86–92).

What is clear is that Bernadette did have a certain fear of Mother Vauzou. And we can see an evolution in the latter's attitude towards Bernadette.

At first her dominant feeling was one of happiness at welcoming 'the privileged child of the Virgin Mary' as she herself told the novices before Bernadette's arrival (B 2, p. 10). One day shortly after Bernadette's arrival, she asked Bernadette to go up to the dormitory early. Then she told her story to the novices and reiterated that they were 'highly favoured to be able to contemplate the eyes that had seen the holy Virgin' (Testimony of Sister Cécile Pagès, B 2, p. 252).

When Bernadette seemed to be on her death-bed and was formally professed (October 1866), Mother Vauzou said: 'We are not worthy to have her, but one must do violence to heaven.'

It was after that crisis, when Bernadette became active again (February 1867), that Mother Vauzou told Bernadette that the period of testing for her was to begin (L 69). Thus the severity was a clear and deliberate decision.

Undoubtedly there was an additional factor involved here: a certain disappointment on Mother Vauzou's part with regard to Bernadette.

'She is just an ordinary nun' said Mother Vauzou. The latter had a demanding conception of holiness that was centred on Christ. So did Bernadette, of course, but the conception of Mother Vauzou had certain mystical and heroic features that were quite alien to the humble pathway of Bernadette. The latter's way was the hidden way of the poor as described in the Gospels (Mt 11:25–27; Lk 10:21–22). It was devoid of great works, magnificent acts, and introspective ruminations. It was grounded rather on pure transparency akin to that of the Virgin Mary, the first and foremost of God's poor and lowly ones. That upset the orientation of Mother Vauzou.

Mother Vauzou did not see Bernadette raised to the altar as a saint. Sister Stanislas Pascal heard her make the following remark, which was accompanied by a 'negative' gesture:

Oh! to lend my voice to the canonization of Bernadette . . .

So long as Mother Vauzou was the Superior General (January 1881 to May 1899), there was no question of introducing Bernadette's cause for canonization in Rome. Mother Joséphine Forestier, who succeeded Mother Vauzou on the top post, was not unaware of this opposition. She came to submit the project of canonization to her.

'Wait until after I am dead', said Mother Vauzou.

What exactly was her complaint against Bernadette? Apparently it was that 'insofar as nature was concerned, Bernadette displayed self-love'. Sister Fabre discussed and debated this evaluation frankly with Mother Vauzou. But she could get 'no other proof' of the charge except the following incident (L 682). One day Bernadette had improvised a little parable-game, which was quite in keeping with her aphoristic bent. She drew a circle on the ground and said: 'Let she who has no self-love put her finger in here' (L 682). When Bernadette put her own finger in to explain the rules, Mother Marie-Thérèse thought that she was holding herself up as an example of someone devoid of pride.

Bernadette certainly had no such intention in mind. Proud, sensitive, and even touchy, Bernadette had a militant concern for justice and was fully aware of being proud (l 683). Indeed she may have been overly conscientious about the matter, as her own words attest frequently (see the word 'pride' in the index to L 3). She knew that she would have to fight against this fault until her dying day.

'I have been rightly told that it will die fifteen minutes after I do', she said to Jeanne Védère (B 1, p. 354).

**The reasons behind Mother Vauzou's harshness**

The reasons behind Mother Vauzou's growing reserve and stiffness towards Bernadette seem quite clear. I should like to discuss them in some detail here.

1. Firstly, she retained a relative amount of scepticism with regard to the apparitions of Lourdes. 'All the same, the rosebush did not blossom', she said to Mother Bordenave.

In 1895 or 1896, she offered two other reasons to Canon Boillot, then the chaplain of the mother-house, after he had just preached a moving sermon about Lourdes:

> There are some bishops who don't believe it (PONev 1228–1229).

She specifically mentioned Bishop Dupanloup of Orléans, but his position is disputed by the various testimonies we have (see L 295). The second reason she gave was this:

> Oh! she was a little peasant girl. . . If the holy Virgin wanted to appear somewhere on earth, why would she choose a common, illiterate peasant instead of some virtuous and well instructed nun? (PONev 1229; B 2, p. 357)

A few days later Canon Boillot expressed his astonishment at Mother Vauzou's view to three nuns on the convent board of directors. They replied frankly:

> Don't you know that our venerable Mother is far from being carried away where Lourdes is concerned? She has spoken to us in very much the same terms (Ibid.).

At the same time, however, we must not oversimplify the matter here. The fact is that she died with Lourdes on her lips:

> She died uttering these words: 'Our Lady of Lourdes,

protect my death-agony' (PANev 337v).

Her reservations were bound up with her classical brand of spirituality. She was not keen on new devotions, apparitions, and special charisms. Her rugged christocentrism (focused on the Sacred Heart) made her mistrust the focus on Mary in popular forms of devotion. In that respect she was ahead of her time. She stood for a point of view that would win out in more recent times.

2. The second reason was the difference in class and social status between Bernadette and herself. Mother Vauzou revealed this bias frequently, as Mother Bordenave and many other witnesses testified:

> I do not understand why the holy Virgin should reveal herself to Bernadette. There are so many other souls more lofty and delicate! Really! (PANev 327–328; other testimony in B 2, pp. 358–359).

3. The third and most decisive reason behind the misunderstandings and stiff relations between Bernadette and herself was undoubtedly the following. She liked to see great openness and frankness of soul in her young nuns.

> She found Bernadette too reserved (PANev 225).

> She ... judged the piety of her novices on the basis of the open revelations they had made to her (Mother Bordenave; PANev 327–328)

Mother Vauzou had doubts about Bernadette's delicacy of heart. 'She told me so herself', Mother Bordenave confirmed (PANev 326). To Mother Villaret she made the following remark about herself and Bernadette:

> Every time that I had something to say to Bernadette, I had the urge to speak harshly... In the novitiate there were other novices to whom I would have gone down

on my knees before I would have done the same to Bernadette (PANev 1123).

This closing-up was mutual. As Father Febvre rightly noticed, Bernadette opened up only to 'naïve people like herself' and to children especially. She 'closed up with persons who were not so simple' (ESB, p. 515).

The situation was made worse by the fact that Bernadette did open herself up more readily to other superiors. Sister Eléonore Cassagnes, in particular, seemed to enjoy her confidence:

Hence a little umbrage in the spirit of Mother Marie-Thérèse Vauzou (PANev 335).

It also happened ... that the venerable (Bernadette) confided her troubles to Sister Nathalie Portant, the second-assistant... Hence a certain amount of hurt feelings (J. Garnier; PANev 1545 v).

In short, Mother Vauzou ran up against not only the simplicity of Bernadette but also the mystery that I have already discussed. It was the mysteriousness of complete transparency, which made her so delightful and admirable in direct conversation and so alien to any analysis of the states of the soul.

4. We must also take into account the impressionable nature of Mother Vauzou, whose ideas were resolute and rather fixed. (B 2, pp. 361–362). She was somewhat conscious of this, and she developed certain scruples about having been too severe with Bernadette. During one of her final retreats in Lourdes near the end of her life, she talked this over with Father Jean Léonard, the Abbot of the Cistercian monastery of Fontfroide. He managed to reassure her on the matter.

'God deigned to let Mother Joséphine Imbert and me be severe for Sister Marie-Bernard, in order to keep her in the ways of humility' (PONev 104v, etc.), said Mother Vauzou, two months before her death.

5. Finally, we must take due note of the artificialities of the time. In those days naturalness, frankness, and limpidity were not appreciated as they are today.

'A stiff, very touchy character,' noted Mother Vauzou about Bernadette in her secret file of the novices. But this remark is compensated for by another, equally confidential, remark: 'Pious, modest, devout; she is orderly' (PONev 324; PANev 334; B2 , p. 364).

The trial was a genuine one for Bernadette, and deeply felt, because the rich personality of Mother Vauzou exercised a real attraction on her novices. She was elected the Superior General of the congregation, and she was regarded as one of the most remarkable nuns of her age.

Bernadette was delighted when Mother Vauzou visited the infirmary. We have already noted how she welcomed her back from a trip with an enthusiasm she later regarded as excessive (L 90). Two factors reinforced this sort of enthusiasm and spirit in the religious community of that era. First of all, girls came into the convent at a youthful age when they had not yet had much experience of life. Secondly, childlike abandonment to their superiors was cultivated in them. Regarding their superiors as representatives of God, the girls projected a halo around them. They saw them as visible signs and transmitters of God's will.

There was also some tension between the official authority vested in the mistress of novices and the charismatic prestige associated with the person of Bernadette. To do justice to Mother Vauzou, we must acknowledge that she never took umbrage at this. Far from trying to destroy or eliminate the other pole of attraction, she was wise enough to recognize it and use it for the benefit of the other novices, as we have seen. She was sufficiently sure of herself, accepted, and strong to feel no worries on that score. And the proverbial docility of Bernadette allowed for a *modus vivendi* which enabled her to exercise her attractiveness in a perfectly controlled way. But there was a certain amount of stiffness on both sides nevertheless.

In Bernadette's case the stiffness was due in part to the

*Mother M. T. Vauzou*        *Mother Joséphine Imbert*

fact that she did not always bend diplomatically as other novices might. Her mission had trained her to stand up to police commissioners, prosecutors, judges, priests, and others.

And yet there was a secret sympathy and a somewhat frustrated attraction between these two women who were so different in many ways. Let me cite one telling indication. When Bernadette was in the infirmary and Mother Vauzou was passing by outside (without going in), the latter would cough as a little signal; and Bernadette would reply with a little cough. This compensatory signalling attests both to their desire to communicate with each other and to the inhibitions which impeded communication (L 281; B 2, pp. 129 and 352).

Now we must delve into the final and ultimate trials that were engraved on the life of Bernadette. They were both physical and moral trials. In the opinion of Sister Marie-Bernard herself, the moral trials were the most formidable and terrible of all.

# 16

# NIGHT AND FOG

From December 12, 1878 to the month before her death, Bernadette would again be subjected to interrogations. This time the circumstances would be particularly trying for her.

## Obstacles encountered by Father Cros

In this case, however, the historian and the friends of truth cannot help but sympathize with those who inflicted this particular trial on Bernadette, even though there were good reason for not bothering her again.

The case of conscience was posed for the first time on August 24, 1878, when Father Cros showed up at Saint Gildard. This Jesuit had been entrusted with the task of writing an accurate, scholarly history of the apparitions. The project had been dear to the hearts of the chaplains of Lourdes ever since Lasserre managed to block their own little history of Lourdes by marshalling Bernadette's objections and sending a printed memorandum to bishops and to the Holy Office in Rome.

Father Cros had been a devoted believer in Lourdes for a long time. He had met Bernadette in 1864 and 1865. Those very first meetings had given him the inspiration to write a history of the apparitions and he had been ready to do it then. If he had, that might have changed the whole story; for his genius as an investigator would undoubtedly have tapped the innermost wellsprings of Bernadette's mind and heart. Unfortunately his superiors ordered him to finish his history of Jean Berchmans first, a figure who was of more interest to the Society of Jesus. So it was only in 1877, after the death of Bernadette's parents and quite a few other witnesses, that he undertook a systematic inquiry among the surviving witnesses of the events in 1858. There were still many around, twenty years after the event. In the spring of 1878, Cros questioned more than two hundred witnesses, including Bernadette's wet-nurse, her companions of February 11 (Jeanne and Toinette), and the miller Nicolau. He vividly recorded their recollections (CROS 1, pp. 509-520).

It was essential that he question the only witness to the apparition: Bernadette. And, sad to say, in 1864 she had herself offered to give her account of it to him, for a certain spark had been lit between them. He had refused at the time, arguing that he believed her well enough without that!

So, on August 24, he came to Saint Gildard in the course of a longer trip. He had already managed to get around a thousand obstacles and to spirit countless unsuspected documents from various files—including those that the former officials of Lourdes in 1858 had improperly concealed. He had met with success everywhere. In Nevers his gallant diplomacy ran up against a stone wall. The nuns had been burnt by the disputes over the earlier books and they feared a new flare-up in the conflict. They now wanted to spare Bernadette this fresh trial, as they had promised to do. The clever keenness of the priest, which had worked wonders so often, only tightened their defences. The nuns referred him to the bishop; the bishop referred him back to the nuns. The run-around got him nowhere.

Cros had managed to win the sympathy of ordinary people. He had won the bishop's valet and the people in the post office to his side. He had asked the latter to let him know about any telegrams because he had asked the bishop of Tarbes to telegraph urgent support for his project. It was all in vain. His last visit to the bishop's valet to obtain some favourable response from the bishop himself was a failure. All he could hear in the distance was 'the shrill, angry voice' of the prelate telling his valet not to let Cros up.

He made a last attempt with the Superior General: 'Pray that the holy Virgin may bend your heart.'

This was the response he got: 'My heart is not bent: it is upright.'

### Cros' appeal to the Pope

It became clear to him that only an order from the Pope himself could resolve the impasse. Cros had outlined his whole proposal as early as November 1877. In November 1878, Archbishop Langénieux of Reims brought it to Rome. On December 8, he announced complete success in his undertaking:

> Leo XIII had signed the papal letter in which he states at the outset that he would be indebted to anyone who would like to help to bring the project to a successful completion ... or to give formal testimony as a witness (CROS, *Récits et mystères*, Toulouse, 1901, p. 12).

So now Bernadette and her superiors had been invited to comply with Father Cros by the Pope himself.

Negotiations were resumed at Saint Gildard. The nuns, however, wanted to see no more of Father Cros himself. They were afraid of his passionately persuasive powers and his ability to pry into things. But they would accept Father Sempé, who was discreet, conciliatory, and modest in his requests when he came to give his side of the earlier dispute with Lasserre in November 1869.

**Questions for Bernadette**

It was Father Sempé who submitted the questions drawn up by Father Cros to Bernadette on December 12, 1878. But her most frequent response to the fifty questions, which were divided into two parts, was: 'I don't remember.'

Uprooting and the passage of time had gradually erased the details in Bernadette's memory. Even as early as a few months after the apparitions, she had begun to forget dates and she could no longer distinguish what happened at a given apparition. The quarrels of the various would-be historians of Lourdes taught her how difficult it was to shed light on the details of events which one cannot go back to for verification. And her honesty can be gauged in the increasing loss of detail in her testimony over the course of time. Contrary to imaginary visionaries, who somehow manage to keep adding details to their message and the event surrounding it, Bernadette never added a word or a fact to her early testimony. She went in for subtraction rather than addition. Having made the apparitions a part of her inner being, she was no longer able to objectify or describe them. She had to summon back her memory from a painfully long distance, and it made her dizzy to gauge it.

And yet certain memories do emerge now and then. Talking to Father Sempé, Bernadette remembered that she found the water 'mild' when she crossed the Gave for the first time to reach the shore of the grotto. (February 11, 1858). She could remember the prayers that she was familiar with at that point in time:

The Our Father, the Creed … in French, and the invocation 'O Mary conceived without sin' (B 2, p. 241).

What was easiest for her to recall were the words of the Virgin in *patois*, and she dictated them once again to Father Sempé.

The next day (December 13) Father Sempé came back and found her 'happy and relaxed'. She recalled a memory from her early childhood:

> Her uncle, the husband of her godmother, returned from Betharram with a few little rings for her play-mates. All the rings were too big for the tiny fingers of Bernadette. She was unhappy about this, but her uncle consoled her by promising that he would bring one that was her size. He kept his word, but now unfortunately the ring was so small that Bernadette could not get it on her finger. Not discouraged, Bernadette used her teeth to finally squeeze the ring on her finger. But now her finger began to swell and cause pain, and both the swelling and the pain got worse. The ring had to be sawed off her finger with a little file.
>
> 'I no longer had any desire for a ring at all', said Sister Marie-Bernard, laughing wholeheartedly (L 535).

Once again Bernadette repeated the words of the apparition and they were taken down. But Cros was not satisfied. There were still problems. He had objections against some of Bernadette's abrupt responses. He was upset by some of her lapses in memory and by certain discrepancies on minute points, most of the latter having to do with correct dates. Bernadette now talked as if all the words had been spoken during one and the same apparition, that of February 18, when Bernadette first heard the lady's voice. Her proverbial stubbornness resisted Father Cros's arguments. Sometimes she was perfectly justified, but sometimes she merely insisted stubbornly on her point of view as she had always done when challenged. The inquiry went on and on as questions poured in from Father Cros, backed up by his weighty arguments.

His requests now came to Nevers with the authority of Leo XIII behind them. Each time the Sisters insisted that this must be the last interrogation. But finally, weary of the struggle, they themselves submitted the new questions to Bernadette with no outside witness present. They did so three times: on January 12, January 30, and March 3, 1879 (L 447–453).

## Dark night all around

These interrogations entailed suffering for Bernadette. Indeed she had made a surprisingly confidential remark to Bishop Bourret of Rodez, when he had insisted on meeting her on September 1, 1877. She told him how reluctant she was to talk about the visions she had seen when she was so young:

> All those things ... are already so far back, so long ago. I no longer remember. I do not like to talk about them too much because, my God, what if I made a mistake! (L 461)

The remark should not astonish us too much. Such forgetfulness and doubt are a classic phenomenon in the case of mystics. It is difficult and often impossible to recall the memory of those states which lasted but a few seconds, of those fleeting moments of extraordinary enlightenment. The Laplanders must find it hard to remember the day-long light of summer during the night-long days of winter. We ourselves often find it hard to imagine that the sun will ever return when it rains day after day.

Thérèse of Lisieux experienced the same eclipse even more keenly. Giving way to vertigo and scrupulosity, she thought that she might have 'lied' after she had recounted the vision of the Virgin that had cured her. Bernadette never gave way to such vertigo. Her basic conviction remained intact always. But she realized that henceforth it would be better for her to focus her attention elsewhere, to concentrate on her day-to-day life and the future that God was gradually nurturing in her. She would be happy 'not in this world but the next', and so she could no longer turn back to her past. In that sense she was already focusing on the future life, and we now view her 'from the back', as it were.

The strength and evident clarity that had sustained her in the face of all her challengers in the past was now evaporating. She could no longer mobilize the lights that had been hers. Like someone blinded in an accident, she could hardly remember what it was like when she could see the light of day.

But that was only a minor aspect of her trial, perhaps the most superficial aspect of all. For now she was going through a twofold dark night of physical suffering and faith.

Cardinal Veuillot, who had expended so much energy in the service of the Church, was crushed under the weight of his final illness. It evoked this surprising remark from him:

> Tell priests not to talk about suffering. Let them not speak about it! They do not know what it is.

Physical suffering is an incomprehensible night. No one can talk lucidly and objectively about it. No one can master it. Bernadette was wise enough to shoulder it humbly, doing a far better job than intellectuals, wise men, and scholars do. She was familiar with these dark tunnels from her many attacks of asthma that brought her to death's door. Yet, in the course of one of these crises, she would say to Julie Garros:

> It is truly painful not to be able to breathe, but it is even more painful to be tortured by interior pains. That is terrible (L 345).

She said that sometime between July and October 1875. That is the first indication she gave of the deeper purifying trial that marked her last years.

She came to appreciate the difference in degree and depth between physical suffering and the deeper suffering that undermined her practice of hope. She sensed the dark shadow of the tempter near her. Her few comments on the matter remind us of the Curé of Ars and Bernanos. During the last few months Sister Tourriol heard her speak to the Spirit of evil firmly, though she was in much pain.

'Go away', she said.

Her lucidity remained amid this dark night. When she learned of Dean Peyramale's death in October 1877, she said:

Oh now it will soon be my turn. But first I must go through *another death* (1 466).

Sister Marthe de Rais bears witness to the same line of thought:

One day I saw her in tears ... I say to her: 'Sister Marie-Bernard, why are you crying? Are you sick?' She replied: 'Oh no! It's not that... If you knew all that was going on inside me... Pray for me' (L 806).

This trial was known about quite early. Father Sempé was to bring the matter up the day after Bernadette's death. Informed about it by Father Sempé, Jean-Baptiste Estrade was to mention it in his *Histoire intime des apparitions*, which was first published in 1898:

In the last years of her life, she was assailed by moral terrors, which were a thousand times worse than her physical sufferings.

Father Febvre, her last confessor, was to specify the most characteristic feature of this inner suffering:

She often reproached herself for not having 'paid back' God for all the graces she had received.

But this trial, too, was immersed in an even more radical dark night of which we get only the most tenuous glimpses. Like Thérèse of Lisieux, Bernadette experienced a dark night of faith. Her life was no longer lit up by light and alluring charms. Her fidelity now was to a hidden and silent God, and it was shaken by the tumult of inner doubts and temptations. Here again we see things only from the back, for we can barely glimpse her still lively freedom amid this apparent collapse.

## The passion of Bernadette

Bernadette's life ended as it had begun: in a 'passion'. In childhood she faced hunger, poverty, and health problems. Now she had to endure sickness, impotence, and both physical and moral darkness. Here the word 'passion' is correct in the strict, etymological sense, as her confessor makes clear in the following remark:

> The *passive* virtues abounded in her: a life of penitence sanctified by God's action ... and fashioned by the cross.

Commenting on God's mysterious work in her, he made the following relevant remark along the same lines:

> It is more that she was worked over than that she herself did the work (ESB, p. 515; B 2, p. 414).

Bernadette shouldered this 'passion' (and she herself used that word) actively and consciously. With every ounce of strength in her, she identified herself with the passion of the crucified Christ. More and more she came to recognize herself in him, though only in a groping way.

'Out Lord was treated like a broken pot', she said as early as 1877 (L 481; B 2, p. 415).

# 17

# THE FINAL MONTHS
# (DECEMBER 1878–APRIL 1879)

From December 11, 1878, Bernadette 'is confined to bed once and for all' (LASSERRE, *Bernadette*, 1879, p. 349). Henceforth she was to get up only to lounge for a while in her armchair with its accompanying foot-rest.

## A vessel of suffering

Father Febvre, an assiduous visitor during these final months gives the following description of her ills:

> Chronic asthma, chest pains, accompanied by spitting up of blood that went on for two years. An aneurism, gastralgia, and a tumour of the knee... Finally, during the last few years she suffered from bone decay, so that her poor body was the vessel of all kinds of pain and suffering. Meanwhile abscesses formed in her ears ... inflicting partial deafness on her. This was very painful for her and ceased only a short time before her death.
>
> After she made her perpetual vows (September 22, 1878), her sufferings redoubled in intensity and ceased only at her death. Her ambition, which she concealed as much as she could, was to be a victim for the Heart of Jesus (L 554).

Bernadette's superiors described in greater detail one of her most obvious ills that greatly concerned the infirmarians attending her:

> Ankylosis of the knee... Terrible pain: a huge knee, impaired leg, which one hardly knew how to move. Sometimes it took an hour to change her position. Her facial expression changed greatly: she became like a corpse. She, who was very energetic in her desire for suffering, was completely vanquished by the pain. Even while sleeping, the least movement of the leg drew a cry of anguish from her ... and these cries prevented her companions in the infirmary from sleeping. She passed whole nights without sleep. In her pain and suffering she shrunk down almost to nothing (shorthand notes of Father Cros, A 1; ESB, p. 516).

### Just 'holding on'

Doctor Robert Saint-Cyr, disconcerted by the ups and downs of the preceding years, was further upset now. He was all the more upset because he would have liked to give her some relief. For he had a high opinion of her, as his earlier evaluation of her work indicated (see p. 190 in this volume). Frustrated by his own impotence, he gradually came to regard her as a 'queer patient'. As a substitute for diagnosis, he would say strange or enigmatic things to her.

'You have a terrible enemy', he said on one occasion.

'With that,' noted Bernadette, 'he turned on his heel. I'm beginning to think he's losing his grip' (Letter of December 28, 1876; ESB, p. 473).

Finally, around the start of 1879, she made a decision: 'I don't want him to come back!' (L 546).

She had such a hard time just 'holding on' that she avoided needless pain and effort. She did not try to rise to the heights of heroic stoicism. She knew that she must remain true to herself and not treat herself harshly. She humbly accepted herself for what she was.

In January 1879, a nun offered her '36 recommendations' while asking her to pray for all sorts of things. Sister Victoire Cassou recounted the incident:

> Bernadette did not give away anything, though at the time she was suffering terribly. On the contrary, she was very gracious to the visitor. But when the Sister had left, she could not help saying: 'I like to see the back of people's heels rather than the tip of their nose. When one is suffering, one needs to be alone.'
>
> I said to her: 'You'll say the same thing about me after I have left.'
>
> 'Oh no, my poor friend, it's not the same thing' (L 545).

In a letter dated January 5, 1879, she tried for the last time to reassure her family:

> I am doing better. I cough less since the weather has grown a little milder (ESB, p. 508).

She said nothing about her knee or her stomach. They were making a novena for her, and so she ends on a hopeful note:

> If I am cured, I would ask all of you to go to the grotto to give prayerful thanks (ESB, p. 508).

### The longest nights

From February 1879 on, she had to have a night attendant to watch her in the Sainte-Croix infirmary: 'her right leg outside the bed, resting on a chair'. The night was filled with pain and continual groans, according to Sister Michel Duhème, one of her attendants during those months (L 551).

It was a kind of muffled moan between clenched teeth, interrupted by brief silences. I knew that she was trying to hold it in for my sake... She was aware that I was staying awake. To obey the assignment I had been given, I said to her at one point: 'My dear Sister, you surely must need something. Can I do something for you?'

'No,' she replied, 'go to sleep, go to sleep. I will call you if I need something.'

I tried to stay still to give her the impression that I was sleeping, but she was not fooled. When I said goodbye to go to prayer, she said:

'You didn't sleep, did you?'

Sister Infirmarian came to tell me that I would not be going back to attend Bernadette. Bernadette herself had told the infirmarian:

'I don't want that Sister to attend me during the night any more ... I want Sisters who go to sleep.' (L 551).

Here we see a final indication that she still has her inner freedom. She still can say: 'I want,' 'I don't want.' She expressed this freedom for the sake of others, and she did it with enough authority to get compliance.

Incapable of stifling certain groans, she told people:

Pardon me for complaining so much (L 555).
Don't take my contortions seriously (L 556).

### An inspiring presence

Contact with her did not depress people, wherever she might be and whatever state she might be in. A little postulant, Camille Labaume, was brought to see her on March 20. Bernadette was practically down and out, but she recovered enough to say:

Mademoiselle, I am in a great deal of pain. I cannot embrace you, but I will pray for you.

She knew how to give a gracious 'thank you' for the 'fine broths' and the good wishes that people conveyed to her:

I am cared for better than a princess (L 563).

On March 19, she informed Father Febvre that she had asked Saint Joseph for 'the grace of a happy death'. She didn't want to hear any more talk about novenas for her:

To pray for my cure, not a bit of it! (L 561)

The chaplain's encouraging words hit the spot and rekindled her hope: 'Oh yes? .. That thought does me good' (L 579). But then she added: 'How long the end is in coming!' (L 578).

**Extreme Unction (March 28, 1879).**

On March 28, they suggested that she should receive the Anointing of the Sick. (This would be at least the fourth time since 1868.)

'I have been cured every time I received it', she protested (L 568).

After receiving viaticum, anointing, and some words of comfort from Father Febvre, Bernadette had a few words to say:

My dear Mother, I ask your pardon for all the pain I have caused you by my infidelities in the religious life, and I also ask pardon of my companions for the many bad examples I have given them ... especially for my pride!

The tone of conviction impressed all of them. Father Febvre noted that it was like the thundering voice of a preacher who wanted to make himself heard and understood (L 569; B 2, p. 269). Then they gave her little commissions to carry out for them in heaven.

'Yes, I won't forget anyone', she replies.

On March 29, Father J. E. Greuzard brought her a photograph of a statue of Our Lady of Lourdes made by Armand Caillat, a celebrated Lyonnais artist.

'It is the least bad', she remarks indulgently. But she could not help adding:

I don't know why people depict the holy Virgin like that. I have always said that she did not hold her head bent back like that. That is not the way she looked at heaven (L 571).

**Giving her all**

At the end of March, Sister Philomène Roques received permission to attend her at night. She heard Bernadette cry out in some painful nightmare.

'What's the matter, dear Sister? Are you in pain?'

'Oh, I was *down there*, and a little boy was throwing stones in the stream', Bernadette answered.

Was it perhaps the stone thrown by Jeanne Abadie that was now resurfacing in her final agonies?

That very morning a draw-sheet had to be placed on her bed. The infirmarian tells us:

Her poor body was just one big sore. There was no skin left on her lower parts (L 472).

As Easter approached, she took advantage of a final remission to decorate an egg. She used a penknife to scratch a decoration on the rose-coloured egg. A bit more like her old self again, she reiterated a little thought that she knew would cheer up her visitors:

Human beings no longer have a heart, so I put one on eggs.

They cut her hair for the last time, as they had been doing periodically for the benefit of various mission works. It provided some money for the ransom of slaves. That explains her reply to Sister Marie Guerre one morning, when the latter took off her bonnet for the morning dressing and found her head shaved:

It's to buy a black woman.

Bernadette never gave less than her all, and she did it with a ready heart.

**Holy Week**

During Holy Week (April 6-13, 1879), the scabs and sores became worse. Bernadette asked for something that would enable her to manage:

If you could find something to relieve my back in your medicine chest. The skin is completely peeled off (L 577).

Look among your drugs ... for something to revive me. I feel so weak I can hardly breathe. Bring me some strong vinegar to sniff (L 577).

The time had come for her to divest herself of everything:

She has all the images around her bed taken away.

'This is enough for me', she says, pointing to her crucifix.

On Monday, April 7, the questions and disputes of the historians came back to her mind. She found the strength to make the following comments to Mother Éléonore Cassagnes:

As for me, I want no disputes. I certainly advised my relatives to stay out of it (L 576).

I have told the events. Let people abide by what I said the first time. I may have forgotten and so may others. The simpler one writes, the better it will be. The passion touches me more when I read it than when someone explains it to me (L 576).

*The Sainte-Croix infirmary where Bernadette died*

# 18

# EASTER FOR BERNADETTE

On Easter Sunday, April 13, Bernadette 'was coughing continuously'. To Sister Saint-Cyr Jollet, she confided the following:

> This morning, after Holy Communion, I asked our Lord for five minutes relief so that I could talk to him leisurely. But he did not choose to give me them. . . *My passion will last until my death.*

**Farewell to Sister Bernard**

On Easter Monday she was visited by Sister Bernard Dalias:

> The curtains had been raised. The patient's face was turned towards the wall, and she did not stir . . . I went to lean over the foot of her bed for a moment to see her one last time.
>
> Then, with one of those childish expressions she had always managed to keep, she opened one eye and looked at me, making a little sign that I was to come closer. . . Her emaciated hand touched mine lightly.
>
> 'Adieu . . . Bernard,' she said to me, 'this time is really the last.'
>
> Prompted by an impulse to venerate her, I was going

to bring her little hand up to my lips; but she very quickly pulled it back under the covers (L 583).

Bernard Dalias was the girl who, when she was introduced to Bernadette for the first time, had said: 'This one here!' (see page 157 in this volume). She now recalled that incident:

> When we first met, Bernadette had extended that same hand to me with a smile. Today she was withdrawing it... Thus our twelve years of tender friendship were enclosed between two handshakes... She did not notice the presence of my companions, so that amounted to the privilege of a personal farewell for me.

**Ground in the mill**

That same Easter Monday she was still putting up a fight. To Sister Cécile Pagès, the house pharmacist, she said:

> Isn't there anything you could find to perk up my spirits ... to help me breathe? (L 584).

> There's no relief for me. Father Chaplain told me that the good God wants me to merit as much as I can while I remain on this earth. I guess I must resign myself.

Her face was flushed, her prostration overwhelming. A childhood memory flitted across her mind.

'I have been ground in the mill like a grain of wheat,' she said to Sister Léontine. 'I would never have thought that one must suffer so much to die' (L 585).

That night (between Easter Monday and Easter Tuesday) she enters a 'spiritual agony'.

'Get away, Satan', her confessor heard her repeat several times. He recounts what happened next:

On Tuesday morning she told me that the devil had tried to frighten her, but that she had invoked the holy name of Jesus and the whole thing had disappeared (L 586).

That same morning she received Holy Communion again; but in the course of the morning she was subjected to a serious crisis of oppression. She had me summoned and asked to receive the sacrament of Penance. Afterwards I gave her the plenary indulgence for the dying. As I was telling her to renew the sacrifice of her life out of love, she interrupted me with surprising liveliness:

'What sacrifice? It isn't a sacrifice to leave a meagre life where one encounters so many difficulties in trying to belong to God (L 587).'

She makes every effort to repeat the invocations I suggest to her. But she says:

'How right the author of the *Imitation of Christ* was in telling people that they must not wait for the last moment to serve God. One is capable of so little!'

At 7.00 p.m. Sister Nathalie came to her bedside. She had a rare gift for making contact with people and a sympathetic presence, gifts which she had developed while working with the deaf.

'My dear Sister, I'm afraid. I have received so many graces and I have profited so little from them', Bernadette told her.

Sister Nathalie encouraged her to offer up 'all the merits of the heart of Jesus'. She promised to help Bernadette to 'thank the holy Virgin right up to the end'. She also added a few words in a low voice. She did not recount what those words were, but she did tell us Bernadette's response:

Ah! I thank you! (L 589)

It was the last time that the sun was to set on Bernadette.

## The last night

That night (April 15–April 16) she was attended by a novice, Sister Alphonse Guerre. The latter recounts what happened:

> I went up to the infirmary around 9.00 p.m., after evening prayers. The dear patient ... answered me gently, feebly. I found her so weary and worn out that I thought it wise not to lie down ... I sat down by her bed to be ready to aid her.
>
> From time to time her suffering wrung a feeble groan from her, and this made me start in my chair. She asked me quite a few times to help her turn over so that she could find a little relief. Her meagre body was almost raw, and you could say that she was resting on her sores.
>
> So the two of us tried to get together and work out this difficult manoeuvre. I took the foot on her bad leg ... and I tried to follow the movements of her body so that she could turn over all at once without having to bend the knee. I noticed that during that interminable night not a word of impatience or dissatisfaction escaped her lips... Everything else has slipped my mind (L 590).

In the morning she was visited by Mother Marie-Louise Bourgeot. Bernadette, still very much present, remembered to give her a picture for one of her nuns in Beaumont: Sister Madeleine Bounaix. At 11:30 a.m. she asked to be helped up from the bed:

> We sat her up in the armchair. She noticed the time when the clock struck ... and asked pardon of the companions around her who have been made late for their midday meal because of her (L 593).

## Her final hours with the crucifix

Mother Éléonore Cassagnes recounts that she kept looking at the crucifix across the room from her armchair (L 593). Between noon and 1:00 p.m. she 'tried to take a little food but did not succeed' (Mother Joséphine Forestier):

> Her state of extreme weakness struck me . . .. I thought it my duty to inform the infirmarian and to alert the community (L 594).

Father Febvre came in, heard her confession once again, and recited the prayers for the dying with her. She repeated his words 'in a feeble but distinct voice' (L 595). Her 'look' was still focused intently on the crucifix hanging on the opposite wall (L 593 II). The chaplain takes up the account here:

> In a quiet moment I offered her encouragement with the biblical words from the Song of Songs (8:8): 'Set me as a seal on your heart.'
>
> We saw her clutch her crucifix and place it on her heart, squeezing it tightly. She wanted it to stay right on that spot. I think someone tied it there to make sure that it would not be shifted by any involuntary movement caused by her pain (L 596).

With this gesture Bernadette apparently sought to seal her covenant with the crucified Jesus. Between 1:30 and 2.00 p.m., Mother Éléonore resumed the conversation with Bernadette.

'You are on the cross.'

Bernadette stretched her two hands towards the crucifix: 'My Jesus! Oh! How much I love you!' (L 597).

At 2:15 p.m. one of her sister nuns resumed the conversation with her:

'My sister, are you suffering a great deal?'

'All that is good for heaven.'

'I am going to ask our Immaculate Mother ... to give you some consolation.'

'No,' says the patient, 'no consolations, only strength and patience' (L 599; deposition of Father Febvre).

Then Bernadette remembered the blessing that Pius IX had granted her for the hour of her death. She wanted to hold the paper in her hands

> to benefit from its actual application. We pointed out to her that this was not necessary, that all she had to do was invoke the name of Jesus and have the proper intention (L 600).

At that moment she tried to raise herself up, putting her right hand on the armchair for support. She looked up to heaven and brought her left hand to her forehead. Her eyes were piercing, and for a few moments they kept staring at some fixed point. Her features expressed calmness, serenity and, at the same time, a certain melancholic gravity. Then, in an indescribable tone of voice, suggesting surprise more than pain, and with ever growing expression, she exclaimed three times: 'Oh! Oh! Oh!' Her whole body trembled (L 601). It was 2:30 p.m.

At 2:55 p.m. the bell rang for the litanies which the community recited daily in the chapel. Bernadette 'wished to take a little rest'. Her confessor and the nuns left her.

'The holy Virgin will come down to meet you', said someone by way of encouragement.

'Oh yes, I hope so', Bernadette replied.

Around 3:00 p.m. the patient seemed to be suffering from some indescribable inner agony. She clutched her crucifix (the one which Bishop de Ladoue brought her from Rome in 1877), contemplated it lovingly for a moment, and then slowly kissed each of Christ's wounds (L 605).

Sister Nathalie, who came in at that moment, found her absorbed in contemplating her crucifix:

Suddenly Bernadette raised her head ... with an indescribable look ...

'My dear Sister, pardon me ... pray for me
... *pray for me*.'

[Sister Nathalie] and the two infirmarians fell on their
knees to pray. The patient joined in their invocations,
repeating them in a low voice (L 606).

Then she recollected herself for a few moments, her
head learning towards the infirmarian on her left. Then,
with an expression of pain and of total abandonment,
she raised her eyes to heaven, stretched her arms to the
cross, and gave out a loud cry: 'My God!' (L 607).

A shudder ran through the three nuns still kneeling
by her side.

Once again Bernadette joined in the prayers being said
by her companions: 'Holy Mary, Mother of God ...'

She came to herself once again and twice repeated the
phrase:

'Holy Mary, Mother of God, pray for me, *poor sinner*'
(L 608).

She looked intently at Sister Nathalie and stretched her
arms out to her. Sister Nathalie, who had worked with the
deaf, did not need words to know what people were trying
to say. Her inquiring look told Bernadette that she knew
Bernadette wanted something of her, though not a word
had been spoken. Bernadette realized that.

'It's that you would help me,' Bernadette said 'in a loud
voice' (L 609).

Sister Nathalie recalled the promise she had made to
Bernadette the evening before: to help her 'thank the holy
Virgin right up to the end'. A few moments later

the patient signed for something to drink. She made a big Sign of the Cross, laid hold of the decanter offered her, took a few sips a couple of times and, lowering her head, gently delivered up her soul (L 611).

Sister Gabrielle de Vigouroux, the infirmarian, entered the room at the last moment:

I arrived just on time to be there when she breathed her last, supported on my arm. She was holding her crucifix in her hand, supporting it on her heart. Someone had even attached it, I think. She was turned on her right side, but she closed her eyes. I recall having had trouble closing her right eye, which opened several times (L 611).

Lasserre saw her in death (notes Zola in his 1892 *Journal de Lourdes*). He says 'that she was very beautiful'.

SAINTE BERNADETTE dans sa Châsse

*Unless a wheat grain drops into the earth and dies, it remains only a single grain; but if it dies it yields a rich harvest.*

*Armchair where Bernadette died*

*How happy my soul was, good Mother,*
*when I had the good fortune to gaze upon you!*
*How I love to recall the pleasant moments spent*
*under your gaze, so full of kindness and mercy for us.*

*Yes, tender Mother, you stooped down to earth*
*to appear to a mere child. . . You, the Queen of heaven and earth,*
*deigned to make use of*
*the most fragile thing in the world's eyes.*

*(Bernadette, Journal dedicated to the Queen of Heaven,*
*1866; ESB, p. 187)*